THE SAMUEL AND ALTHEA STROUM LECTURES IN JEWISH STUDIES

Make Yourself a

TEACHER

RABBINIC TALES OF MENTORS AND DISCIPLES

Susan Handelman

UNIVERSITY OF WASHINGTON PRESS

Seattle and London

UNIVERSITY OF WASHINGTON PRESS
PO Box 50096, Seattle, WA 98145, USA
www.washington.edu/uwpress

LIBRARY OF CONGRESS CATALOGING-IN-PUBLICATION DATA
Handelman, Susan A.
Make yourself a teacher : rabbinic tales of mentors and disciples / Susan Handelman.
      p. cm. — (The Samuel and Althea Stroum lectures in Jewish studies)
Includes bibliographical references and index.
ISBN: 978-0-295-99128-3 (hardcover : alk. paper)
ISBN: 978-0-295-99129-0 (pbk. : alk. paper)
1. Teacher-student relationships in rabbinical literature.
2. Teacher-student relationships—Religious aspects—Judaism.
3. Eliezer ben Hyrcanus.
4. Jewish learning and scholarship.
5. Rabbinical literature—History and criticism.
6. Spiritual life—Judaism.
I. Title.
BM496.9.T43H36 2011   296.1′206—dc23   2011024354

SAMUEL STROUM, businessman, community leader, and philanthropist, by a major gift to the Jewish Federation of Greater Seattle, established the Samuel and Althea Stroum Philanthropic Fund.

In recognition of Mr. and Mrs. Stroum's deep interest in Jewish history and culture, the Board of Directors of the Jewish Federation of Greater Seattle, in cooperation with the Jewish Studies Program at the University of Washington, established an annual lectureship at the University of Washington known as the Samuel and Althea Stroum Lectureship in Jewish Studies. This lectureship makes it possible to bring to the area outstanding scholars and interpreters of Jewish thought, thus promoting a deeper understanding of Jewish history, religion, and culture. Such understanding can lead to an enhanced appreciation of the Jewish contributions to the historical and cultural traditions that have shaped the American nation.

The terms of the gift also provide for the publication from time to time of the lectures or other appropriate materials resulting from or related to the lectures. A full listing of the books in the series can be found at the end of the book.

For Jerome Katzin, in honor of a life of giving and caring

Yehoshua ben Perahyah would say: "Make yourself a teacher, acquire a friend, and judge everyone favorably."

—*Pirkei Avot* 1:6

"Make yourself a teacher" – This means, even if this person is not on the level to be your teacher, still . . . make him your teacher, to the extent that you imagine him teaching. That way wisdom will come to you. For learning by oneself is not as valuable as learning from another. Solitary learning is good, but learning with another is better, and more clearly retained, even if the other is on the same intellectual level or beneath yours.

—Maimonides, Commentary on *Pirkei Avot*

"Acquire a friend" . . . How so? This teaches that a person should acquire a friend with whom to eat, drink, study Scripture and Mishnah, sleep and reveal all his secrets, the secrets of Torah and the secrets of worldly things.

—*Avot de-Rabbi Natan* 8:3

Said R. Hiyya bar Abba: "Even the parent and child, the teacher and disciple who study Torah at the same gate become enemies of each other. And they do not move from there until they come to love each other."

—*Kiddushin* 30a-b

[The teacher/student relation] is not circumscribed by language or text. It is a fact of life between generations. It inheres in all training and transmission be it in the arts, in music, in crafts, in the sciences, in sport or military practice. Impulses towards loving fidelity, towards trust, towards seduction and betrayal are integral to the process of teaching and apprenticeship. The eros of learning, of imitation and subsequent enfranchisement is as susceptible to crises, to ruptures as is that of sex.

—George Steiner, *Lessons of the Masters*

Every person must find oneself a teacher from among the living, and a teacher from among the great ones in the World of Truth.

—R. Simhah Bunem of Przysucha

CONTENTS

PREFACE

But all this that can and should be known is not really knowledge!
Teaching begins when the subject matter ceases to be subject matter
and changes into inner power.

—Franz Rosenzweig

T HE title of this book is taken from a famous ancient rabbinic saying,
"Make yourself a teacher, acquire a friend, and judge everyone favorably" (*Pirkei Avot* 1:6). It originated in a series of three talks I delivered at the University of Washington, Seattle, in April 2004: the Twenty-Ninth Annual Samuel and Althea Stroum Lectures in Jewish Studies. These lectures were endowed through the generosity of the Stroum family. I thank the family and the university's Jewish Studies Program for honoring me with their invitation, which gave me a forum to present my ideas, and for their support in publishing this volume. This book is an expanded version of those lectures.[1]

Like all academics, I bear the twin obligations of scholarship and teaching, but the latter can suffer due to the demands of the former. By mid-career, I had completed two books on literary theory and Jewish thought, edited others, and become a tenured professor. I was also an avid student of Torah and Jewish tradition—and someone very concerned about contemporary education. I felt an urgent need to bring all these parts of my life together, to understand more deeply what it is I do every time I stand before a class. I also found that I am always in the process of making myself a teacher: each new day, each new class, each new semester brought its challenges, surprises, and need for change.

Interestingly, *"aseh lekha rav,"* the Hebrew version of the rabbinic saying "Make yourself a teacher," is grammatically ambiguous. It can also be read, "Make *for* yourself a teacher." Maimonides, the great medieval Jewish philosopher and commentator interprets these words to mean you should "imagine" the other as your teacher. But if you "imagine" the other person as your teacher, are you then relating to her or him simply as an object, a means to access your own intellect?[2] What indeed is it that we do when we teach? And what does it mean to say that texts teach us something? What is the relation of knowledge, spirituality, and education in our time? How can university learning be bettered? And what might Jewish models of study and commentary have to say about the way we teach and learn?

I sympathize with Jane Tomkins, another literary theorist who became intensely interested in pedagogy later in her career. Tomkins has written that despite our professed academic goals of critical thinking, social change, transmission of cultural heritage, or professional training,

> I have come to think that teaching and learning are not preparation
> for anything but are the thing itself. . . . The classroom is a microcosm
> of the world; it is the chance we have to practice whatever ideals we
> cherish. The kind of classroom one creates is the acid test of what it is
> one really stands for. And I wonder, in the case of college professors,
> if performing their competence in front of other people is all that that
> amounts to in the end.[3]

The original audience to whom I delivered these lectures came from the Seattle Jewish Community and the University of Washington. From the mass of material I had accumulated over the years, I chose a few short, dramatic rabbinic stories about teachers and students. I picked stories that I hoped would engage even those who did not have much specialized knowledge of Jewish tradition, Hebrew, or literary theory. These stories also describe paradigmatic moments in the lives of students and teachers: finding one's teacher, becoming a teacher oneself, and ending one's career as a teacher. These three stories then became the organizational principle of this book.

The intended audience for this work is a general one not limited to academic specialists. I hope that I have been able to draw the general reader into the enchanting world of these classical Jewish texts and achieved some new insight even for specialists. I especially hope that this work will serve as a resource for Jewish and non-Jewish educators on all levels and in many kinds of schools. "There's not really so much need for teachers anymore," since so much material is online, a student at a large American state university was recently quoted as saying.[4] May this book help counter that opinion and inspire educators to be renewed and think further about the deeper meanings of teaching and learning, and our mutual endeavor, which Sigmund Freud once called "the impossible profession."

I especially wish to thank several of my extraordinary teachers and friends in Jerusalem with whom I have shared the joys of Jewish learning: Rav Marc Kujavski, Yardena Cope-Yosef, Melila Eshed-Hellner, Josianne Parig, Simi Peters, Phyllis Platt Jesselson, Gilla Rosen, Esther Sha'anan, Barbara Sofer, and Noam Zion. I am particularly indebted to Ora Wiskind-Elper, Jeffrey Saks, and Robert Eisen—each a superb teacher, scholar, and colleague. Each read the entire manuscript carefully, stimulated my thinking, offered wonderful insights, and saved me from errors. My editor at the University of Washington Press, Beth Fuget, has been a faithful coach, gentle critic, and patient midwife and helped deliver this book safely from the throes of its many birth pangs. Michal Michelson and Karen Marron were my meticulous and superb copy editors in Israel who worked graciously under stressful deadlines. Japhet Johnstone was the extraordinary copy editor to whom my manuscript was fortunately assigned by the University of Washington Press. His devotion and expertise have made this a much better book. Thanks to the book designer Tom Eykemans, to whom I am also grateful for the creative cover, and to managing editor Marilyn Trueblood and other Press staff members for their unflagging support of this work. Rachel Adelman generously shared her abundant wisdom on bibliography and rabbinic texts. Smadar Wisper of the Bar-Ilan University English Department Seminar Library was an expert Sherlock Holmes, always happy and always willing and able to help track sources and find material.

I also thank Bar-Ilan University for the year of sabbatical leave I was given to complete this manuscript. Over that year, I watched the trees outside the window above my desk turn from deep green to yellow, to black, and then slowly back to green. As the year turns once more, it is time to send this book into the world, let it find its audience, and hope it will do some good.

Rosh Hashana, Jerusalem, 2011

Postscript: As this book went into production, my dear mother, Marian Handelman (Miryam bat Freyda ve-Shemuel haCohen Katzin) passed away on May 5, 2011, after an illness of several months, during which I was by her side. As a close friend wrote, "It was a blessing to be able to perform the special mitzvah of honoring one's parents in those months. But most of all, you have been blessed to have a mother whose love you have always felt, and about whom you can truly say, *"immi, morati"* [my Mother, my Teacher]. She was indeed my best teacher, epitomized by the verse from Proverbs 31:26, "She opens her mouth with wisdom, and the Torah of kindness is on her tongue."

A NOTE ON TRANSLATION
AND TRANSLITERATION OF HEBREW

I have consulted several sources when translating Hebrew texts into English, including the Soncino editions of the Talmud and Midrash, and the Jewish Publication Society translation of the Bible. When using these sources, however, I have made my own minor modifications in the grammar, syntax, punctuation, and word choice to clarify literary points. Hebrew and French texts that have not been translated, I have done on my own. I have used the standard printed editions of rabbinic texts, except where noted.

Most of the Hebrew words in this book have been transliterated according to the "general" transliteration system in the *Encyclopaedia Judaica*, with the following exceptions: I make no distinction between the Hebrew letters "ה" (hei) and "ח" (het) and use the letter "h" for both. I use "tz" to denote the letter "צ" (tzaddi).

I have also written the Hebrew names of people, places, and texts according to the spellings appearing in the *Encyclopaedia Judaica*, and the Jewish Publication Society's recent transliteration guide. Although the *Encyclopaedia Judaica* tends to use the common English forms of Hebrew surnames (e.g., "Joshua" instead of "Yehoshua"), I preferred to transliterate most Hebrew surnames. I did use the English forms in certain cases, e.g., "Moses" and "Elijah the Prophet." I use the abbreviation "R." to signify the title "Rabbi." In some of the primary texts, the word "Rabban" is used as a title, for example for R. Yohanan and R. Gamaliel. The title was used for the *Nasi*, president of the Jewish High Court.

NOTES ON NOTES

I have tried to curb the academic disposition to ply each page with footnotes detailing internal scholarly debates and references, and left much of that for the bibliography. There remain, though, the many notes needed for accurate documentation of the sources I cite in the text. Notes may often include citations, extended quotations, added commentary, references, and/or linguistic background. For the reader interested in probing further, I have added several longer expository notes.

The Talmud is cited in the standard way by Hebrew tractate and folio page. For instance, *Hagigah* 3b means the tractate named "Hagigah," page 3, side or folio b of this page. The citation *Gittin* 56 a-b means the text is found across both sides of page 56. Unless otherwise specified, the Talmudic citations refer to the Babylonian and not the Jerusalem Talmud. The Mishnah, the compilation of ancient rabbinic oral law upon which the Talmud comments, is cited by Hebrew tractate name, chapter, and specific law, e.g., *Kelim* 2:1 means the tractate called "Kelim" [or "Vessels"] chapter 2, law number 1. Midrashic collections commenting on the Bible and available in English translation, such as Midrash Rabbah, follow the Soncino edition reference system. Other rabbinic texts unavailable in English follow the systems unique to the varying edition used and so cannot be standardized.

I use the full personal names of classic rabbinic commentators along with the acronyms by which they are known in Jewish tradition. For example, Rabbi Moshe Hayyim Luzzatto is known as "Ramhal," an abbreviation composed of the first letters of his name. Other commentators are known by titles of books they have written, or phrases taken from the Bible. A case in point is R. Yosef Hayyim ben Eliyahu al-Hakham of Baghdad who is commonly known as "Ben Ish Hai," the title of one of his classic works, itself a phrase which he took from the biblical verse 2 Samuel 23:20.

MAKE YOURSELF A TEACHER

INTRODUCTION

"I ONLY WANT THE PIECE WHICH IS IN YOUR MOUTH"

Already in my lifetime, I need disciples. If my books do not act as bait, they will have failed in their intent. The best, the essential, can be communicated only *from one human being to another*.

—Friedrich Nietzsche

Just as a plant reproduces and multiplies, so words of Torah reproduce and multiply.

—*Hagigah* 3b

Literature is written only for the sake of those who are in the process of development, and of that in each of us which is still developing. Hebrew, knowing no word for "reading" that does not mean "learning" as well, has given this, the secret of all literature away. For it is a secret, though a quite open one, to these times of ours—obsessed and suffocated as they are by education—that books exist only to transmit that which has been achieved to those who are still developing.

—Franz Rosenzweig

THE author of those eloquent words, Franz Rosenzweig (1886–1929), abandoned his brilliant career in the German university to found an informal institute for adult Jewish education in 1920 in Frankfurt called "The Free Jewish House of Teaching." He died all too soon from Lou Gehrig's disease. But he continued to write, translate and teach even as his physical capacity diminished solely to the ability to blink his eye. Today he is considered one of the greatest Jewish philosophers of the twentieth century.

I sympathize with Rosenzweig's departure from the suffocating German academy of his time to become another kind of "teacher." I am not ready, though, to abandon my career as a professor, but I do hope university learning can be improved, and I believe that Jewish models of study and commentary have much to say to educational reform. I also take with me from Jewish tradition a deep-rooted sense of teaching and learning as "holy" and "redemptive" endeavors; of being bound to a four-thousand-year-old community of memory, hope, study, and practice which has endured the vicissitudes and traumas of history.

I wrote this book in the city of Jerusalem during a time when bombs exploded the buses, cafés, and people on my street, in my university, and throughout the country. These events linked me ever more deeply to the rabbinic Sages about whom I was writing: R. Yohanan ben Zakkai, R. Eliezer ben Hyrcanus, R. Yehoshua ben Hananiah, R. Akiva. All lived in the first two centuries of the Common Era, under the brutal Roman occupation of the Land of Israel. They faced the destruction of Jerusalem, war, and ruthless slaughter. Yet out of destruction and death they re-created life. They were builders of Torah and erected the foundations of rabbinic Judaism, which enabled the Jewish people to survive and flourish in 2,000 years of exile. They taught—and continue to teach—Jews and all those in search of wisdom how to endure and renew amidst catastrophe. I realized anew as I was writing, how much they too were teaching in a time of terror and I gained strength from them.

The Rabbis also understood, as Rosenzweig put it, that "books exist only to transmit that which has been achieved to those who are still developing." In Hebrew, the word for "reading," *keri'ah*, is also the word for "calling." Reading is not just a matter of textual, cultural, or intellectual analysis. It is a voicing, a calling out, a being called to account, a summons to be present, to be transformed. It is also an act of endearment and union. That too, I believe, is what teaching is about.

ORAL TORAH AND WRITTEN TORAH

Jews are not so much the "People of the Book" (Islam affixed that epithet to the Jews) as they are the "People of the Mouth"—of the "Oral Torah" or *Torah she-be-al peh.* The Hebrew word "Torah" itself means "instruction, teaching." It comes from the Hebrew root, *yod, reish, hei* meaning "to cast" or "to shoot"—as in "to shoot an arrow." In one form, the verb means "to aim, direct toward" and then acquires the sense of "to instruct, show the way." *Written* Torah usually refers to the biblical corpus. *Oral* Torah signifies the rabbinic debates, laws, commentaries, stories compiled over thousands of years—even the freshest insight a teacher or student or reader might have this very moment. The three stories upon which I focus in this book come from the Oral Torah.

I spent a great deal of intellectual energy in my previous books, *Fragments of Redemption* and *The Slayers of Moses*, trying to philosophically understand the depths of rabbinic interpretation and its wondrous exegetical extravagances. I sought the origins of that deep creativity, that living pulse of Torah, and wanted to locate where it was still beating today. I connected this interpretive virtuosity to the creativity of contemporary, secularized Jewish thinkers from Freud to Derrida. But I missed the key pedagogical link: Oral Torah attains its creative and interpretive freedom because it is a live, generative teaching, a meeting between teachers and students; it is not only or primarily a "text" sitting on a page. So in this book, my subject is Oral Torah as a mode of learning, one which also involves the deeply personal relation between teacher and student, colleague and colleague.[1]

Moshe Idel, the foremost living academic expert on Jewish mysticism, has noted that in much Jewish thought, even "the book" itself is only one step in a long trajectory of performative religiosity. Learning is instrumental and "knowledge" (though of course important) not its ultimate purpose. Modern Jewish scholarship marginalized this notion of Jewish learning as something experiential, transformative, and intended to reach beyond the strictly intellectual level. This marginalization was partially due to the culture of the nineteenth-century German university in which academic Jewish Studies were born—that same academic culture that Rosenzweig himself eventually left. [2]

Idel also perceptively notes how traditional Jewish modes of learning attempt to bring people together into what he calls a "sonorous community," or "sound community." The text is activated by being sounded out orally, loudly vocalized, or sung. In part, this practice rests on the view that language mediates the experience of God, and so words become forms of power. Singing and sounding out the holy texts also creates an external reality bringing together all who study (just as God creates in the Bible by "calling"—*keri'ah*—not by fiat). Jewish "learning," Idel sums up, is "entering an ambience as much as it is an acquiring of knowledge."[3]

Before approaching the three rabbinic stories I've chosen and entering their ambience, let's pause and probe a bit more deeply the difference between Written and Oral Torah and its significance for the teacher/student relation. R. Joseph B. Soloveitchik (1903–1993), luminary of the highly rationalistic Brisker school of Talmudic interpretation, modern Jewish thinker and educator, describes it in elevated philosophical and psychological terms:

> The act of a master teaching Torah to his students is a wondrous
> metaphysical fact of the revelation of the influencing personality to
> the one influenced by it. This revelation is also the cleaving of teacher
> and student to each other. The student who understands the concept
> cleaves to the intellect that transmits the concept. If he grasps the
> teacher's logic, then he becomes joined to the teacher in the unity of
> the conceiving intellect [*maskil*] and the conceived ideas [*muskal*].
>
> Within this fundamental principle is hidden the secret of the
> Oral Torah, a Torah which by its nature and application can never be
> objectified, even after it has been written down. "Oral Torah" means
> a Torah that blends with the individual's personal uniqueness and
> becomes an inseparable part of man. When the person then transmits
> it to someone else, his personal essence is transmitted along with it.[4]

Reuven Ziegler, an expositor and editor of R. Soloveitchik's writings, underscores the "prophetic element" in R. Soloveitchik's writings on this subject:

> The personality of the master teacher, like that of the prophet, sponta-
> neously overflows toward the student in an act of self-revelation. This
> leaves an indelible impression upon the student's soul and binds the
> two together intimately. In fact, the entire enterprise of the *masorah*
> (passing on the tradition) is based on the unity of teacher and student.[5]

In the rabbinic imagination, God and Moses are the paradigm of this relation but also study partners! The biblical narrative in the book of Exodus concludes the scene of God's revelation at Sinai by saying: "And he gave to Moses, when he finished talking with him upon Mount Sinai, two tablets of Testimony, tablets of stone, written by the finger of God" (Exod. 31:18).

Artistic portrayals of this scene often show a passive, silent Moses receiving tablets from a hand coming down from heaven. The Rabbis, however, focus intently on the phrase "when he finished talking with him." Here they characteristically find more than just a simple marker of chronological time. Instead, the phrase "talking *with* him" "teaches that Moses heard from the mouth of God, [*mi-pi ha-Gevurah*] and they studied and went over the law together" (Midrash *Tanhuma*, "Ki Tissa" par. 16).

The Rabbis further elevate the Oral Torah over the Written, seeing in the former—not the latter—the key to the special relation of God and Israel. The Talmud declares there were words of revelation given to be written and words given not to be written (*Gittin* 60a). When Moses ascends to Sinai to receive the Ten Commandments, the Bible relates, "And the Lord said to Moses, 'Write these words. For according to these words [*al-pi ha-devarim ha-eleh*] I have made a covenant with you and with Israel'" (Exod. 34:27). "According to [these words]" is the natural colloquial translation of the Hebrew preposition *al-pi*, which more literally means "by the mouth." The Talmud interprets: "Rabbi Yohanan said: 'God made a covenant with Israel only for the sake of the Oral Torah, as it says, 'for by the mouth' [*al-pi*] of these words I have made a covenant with you and with Israel'" (*Gittin* 60b).

Now that small piece of rabbinic exposition already gives us a feel for the audacity, creativity, and immediacy of Oral Torah. It is taught in the personal name of the individual Sage who makes the statement: "Rabbi Yohanan said. . . . " Like the other passages I cited above, it startles us, shocks us out of linear, literal, conventional meanings. Oral Torah is not just a set of "texts," but a way of learning, a close personal relation of teacher and student, God and Israel. And Oral Torah is literally sounded. Anyone who today enters a *beit midrash* (house of study) of a traditional Jewish school is immediately surrounded by clamorous noise, quite unlike a hushed university library.[6] One of the traditional modes of study still quite alive in *yeshivot* (advanced Jewish religious academies) is to learn orally in face-to-face intimate dialogue with a fixed study partner (*havruta*), with whom one sits over a table, vocalizes the text aloud, line by line, and argues vigorously about its meaning.[7] These study pairs mutually teach and learn from each other, simultaneously repeat and renew the Word.

R. Léon Askénazi, a contemporary French-Jewish thinker and educator (d. 1996), proposes the following explanation of Oral and Written Torah. There are two kinds of words: the words of tradition set down in writing that have an atemporal "eternal essence" (e.g., the Bible, Written Torah);

and the words of tradition not put into writing that correspond to the development of spiritual life in historical time (Oral Torah). That is, the "Word of God" was first a "word," and only secondarily put in writing. The difference, then, between the "Written" and "Oral" Torahs, he adds, is that "the oral tradition allows us to say this word as word."

What might he mean? Written words lie silently before the reader, fixed letters on the page. Spoken words emerge from the exhalations of our own breath. The sounds vibrate and flow across space from my mouth to the ear of the one to whom I am addressing them, in a unique, non-repeatable moment. "To say the word as word" in Oral Torah, R. Askénazi seems to imply, recaptures the prophetic personal immediacy of God's Word, mouth to ear, face to face, at any moment, and in all the personal and historical situations with which we grapple. Christianity by contrast, he argues, sees itself as having received the "Old Testament" via Israel as the Word of God in the form of a book—not as oral word. The term "Scripture" then takes on a signification in Christian culture that it does not have in Judaism. In fact, the Hebrew term which would be equivalent to the English word "Scripture" is not "Torah," but "Mikra"—meaning "what is put in writing in order to be read." One needs to be precise and not confuse "Torah" and "Mikra," a distinction which is lost when these word are translated into other languages and cultures.[8]

It is then not surprising that Islam also gave the epithet "People of the Book" to the Jews, but the term is inaccurate. Jews, as R. Askénazi writes, "are not the People of the Book . . . and God did not choose a people of readers, nor of libraries. . . . [Rather, they are] the people of the word of One who gave this 'word' to be put in writing in a book." His distinction is subtle but important. It is also a warning to guard against the "idolatry" of writing and the kind of teaching and learning which that would imply.

The Rabbis originally forbade writing down Oral Torah, but for later historical reasons—fear of forgetting and desire to conserve a common, unanimous reference—allowed it. But they edited and set it down in an intentionally different style from the Written Torah. Its rhetorical form intentionally retains its primary "orality"; and so, a page of Talmud or Midrash is not simply and directly "readable" but often seems hermetic. As we'll find, to grasp even a few lines requires lengthy and patient study. One must master a great deal of preliminary technical and methodological information and exert one's creative intellect. But this style is necessary; it also keeps Oral Torah living and in a constant process of elaboration.[9]

Unlike a book, the Oral Torah never finishes. And there are powerful pedagogical consequences, as R. Askénazi also notes: learning this kind of text
also requires an "oral initiation" which comes from a personal relation to a
teacher, who has received oral meanings him- or herself, inner keys to the
text. This teacher, in turn, has undergone initiation by a teacher and so on
backwards through the generations—and then forwards as the Torah is
renewed for the present and future.[10]

TORAH OF THE MOUTH

The following rabbinic interpretation from a midrash on the verse from
Exodus 31:18 simultaneously defines *and performs* what the Oral Torah is
about, using a daring parable:

> Another explanation of, "And he gave to Moses, when he finished talk-
> ing with him upon Mount Sinai, two tablets of Testimony, tablets of
> stone, written by the finger of God" [Exod. 31:18]. . . . It is written "For
> God gives wisdom [*hokhmah*]. Out of His mouth comes knowledge
> [*da'at*] and discernment [*tevunah*]" [Prov. 2:6].
>
> Wisdom is great, but greater still is knowledge and discernment.
> So God gives wisdom. But to him whom He loves, "out of His own
> mouth" comes knowledge and discernment. . . .
>
> R. Yitzhak and R. Levi discussed this verse. One said: "It can be
> compared to a rich man who had a son. The son came home from
> school and found a platter of food in front of his father. His father
> took a piece and gave it to him . . . but the son said: 'I only want the
> piece which is in your mouth.' The father gave it to him from his own
> mouth, because he was so beloved.
>
> . . . Another explanation of "For God gives wisdom": You find that
> when Israel stood ready to receive the Torah on Mount Sinai, they
> wanted to hear the Ten Commandments from God's own mouth. R.
> Pinhas ben Hama, the priest, said: "Two things did Israel ask of God—
> to see His likeness and to hear from His own mouth the Decalogue, as
> it says, 'Let him kiss me with the kisses of his mouth' [Song of Songs
> 1:2]." (Midrash *Exodus Rabbah* 41:3)

Eating and kissing—giving from the "mouth"—also signify deep love and
intimacy, and a teaching that is not external, not just spoken with the lips

or read on a page, but coming from even further "inside the mouth," "spirit to spirit," "breath to breath," inner soul to inner soul. R. Hayyim of Volozhin interprets this midrashic parable in kabbalistic terms, relating it to the larger metaphysical question of how God connects to the world. Is the world found "inside" God? In other words, is God the world's "place," (*makom*)—and the world "swallowed inside God" and connected to His essence? Or is the world "outside" God, and we grasp only the point at which God contracts Himself to connect to the world? The son in the parable wants a Torah connected to the "root" of things, not an external one— he wants an inner relation to God. This, in part, is the difference between speech, which externalizes thought and comes from the lips—an external part of the face—as opposed to what comes from a deeper level "inside the mouth," the "kiss" of mouth to mouth, breath to breath.[11]

So in Oral Torah, teacher and student are also lovers of the Torah, as intimate with it as are husband and wife—and through Torah, lovers of each other and God. Their task, like that of husband and wife, is to "create generations," to give birth, to generate more Torah, more love, and the redemption of the world that flows from its study and practice. Some kabbalistic and Hasidic sources even discuss the intimate relation of student and teacher in terms of "soul impregnation" (*ibbur*).

In academia, we often forget a simple truth: that one needs to love texts in order to read them well, just as we need to love other people in order to understand them well. We focus much more on the necessity of instilling rigorous critical thinking. How can a professor in the secular academic realm also speak of "love" in education without sounding clichéd or simplistic? In a 1958 essay on "The Crisis in Education," the eminent German-Jewish refugee scholar, Hannah Arendt, expressed it this way: "Basically, we are always educating for a world that is or is becoming out of joint." This "is the basic human situation" for every generation because "the world . . . is irrevocably delivered up to the ruin of time, unless human beings are determined to intervene, or alter, to create what is new." She continues,

> Education is the point at which we decide whether we love the world
> enough to assume responsibility for it, and by the same token save it
> from that ruin which, except for renewal, except for the coming of the
> new and young, would be inevitable. And education, too, is where we
> decide whether we love our children enough not to expel them from
> our world and leave them to their own devices, nor to strike from their

hands their chance of undertaking something new, something unfore-seen by us, but to prepare them in advance for the task of renewing a common world.[12]

Arendt herself came from an assimilated German-Jewish background. Though steeped in Western culture and a brilliant philosopher, she did not possess fluency in the classical sources of Judaism. She was deeply involved, though, in questions of Jewish politics and identity, especially after her escape from Nazi Germany to America. But I sense in Arendt's words, a particularly Jewish sense of ever-present possibility of renewal through birth and generation, amidst ever-present possibility and experience of disaster. And a very Jewish sense of how deeply the parent/child relation is intermeshed with the teacher/student relation.

METHODOLOGY: "THE FIGURE IN THE CARPET"

Oral Torah brings us face-to-face with all the teachers in Jewish tradition and makes us their students. In the next chapters, I'll introduce some of the most famous teachers and students, founders of the Oral Torah itself. Chapter 1 discusses one of the most poignant rabbinic stories of a student's struggles to find a teacher and the teacher's spiritual birthing of that student: the story of R. Eliezer ben Hyrcanus and his teacher R. Yohanan ben Zakkai. Chapter 2 revisits one of the most commented upon stories in all rabbinic literature: the dramatic and traumatic argument of this same R. Eliezer ben Hyrcanus with his colleagues over the oven of Akhnai. This incident culminates in R. Eliezer's banning and tragic isolation from his colleagues and students. Chapter 3 explores the poignant scene of R. Eliezer on his death bed, as his colleagues and students return to visit him in a tense, final encounter. These chapters roughly follow the life-cycle of teacher/student relations: becoming a student, finding one's teacher, becoming a colleague and teacher, departing and leaving one's students to carry on.

The teacher/student relations encountered in rabbinic literature are as variegated and unpredictable as all human relations. Of the thousands of stories told, I have chosen just these few which represent themes I wanted to address. I make no pretence to a full examination of the genre, or a history of the subject. In addition to these rabbinic stories from the *aggadah* (the narrative, non-legal parts of rabbinic literature), the *halakhah* (the corpus of rabbinic legal deliberation) contains lengthy discussions of the teacher/student relationship. And in addition to all that material is the vast treasure of Hasidic and kabbalistic literature, marked by special intensity in the expression of love and the connection between mentor and disciple.

I've said that my focus is the teacher/student relationship, but as the reader will find, these stories and my discussions of them will involve other themes as well. Many passages I analyze, for example, will also focus on colleague-colleague relationships; tensions arise between the Rabbis not only because they are colleagues of each other, but also because they are teachers and students of each other. Moreover, as I studied and reread these stories, I came to deeply appreciate how intricately they were composed, how their form and content so beautifully meshed, how allusive and elusive they are. As in a beautiful tapestry, the various threads are intricately interwoven. So my method here is to read the stories as a literary whole. To do that, it is often necessary to pursue what might at first seem an extraneous or unrelated theme or idea. My reader might sometimes feel as if he or she has lost the thread of the tapestry or "figure in the carpet," to use the title of the Henry James story of 1896, where a famous author dies without having conveyed to the world the secret idea that links all his books. But on a deeper level, Talmudic texts themselves often operate by means of rhetorical "digression"—scattering meanings in nonlinear ways, which one then has to patiently trace and rethread.[13] Or as Polonius puts it so well in act two of *Hamlet*: "By indirection find direction out."

Furthermore, as I read and reread these stories, researched, pondered, wrote and rewrote, I found they were also less didactic than I had thought. I had indeed hoped to emerge with various conclusions and prescriptions about the teacher/student relation. But I found that these sophisticated literary and religious texts confront us with the complexity and ambiguity of life itself and of all intimate human relations. The stories do not always lead to clear positions, prescriptions, or conclusions one could write up as in an education textbook.

So, many times I will leave my readers with more questions than answers. But that, too, is a part of the experience of engaging Talmudic texts, part of their own self-conscious "pedagogy." In chapter 3, I cite the philosopher Emmanuel Levinas's comment about this Talmudic style in the context of the narrative of R. Eliezer's death. This story's full sense, he writes, is acquired only through the way the Talmud amplifies the original problem it poses: the meaning comes "by the new questions its own questions will raise, and by the non-spoken meanings that will appear in the meaning it expresses."[14] That process is a fundamental mode of Jewish learning; and I would like to think that this book not only is *about* Jewish models of teaching and learning, but also *enacts* them. R. Shlomo Carlebach, a contemporary Hasidic teacher, spoke of the way one of his own great teachers, R. Shlomo Heiman, would deal with questions. When R. Carlebach would pose a difficult question, often his teacher would not answer. The other students would say, "Rabbi, you are not answering!?" R. Heiman would respond: "Where is it written in the Torah that one has to answer every question and solve every difficulty?" And often he would add, "The question is so good—why ruin such a good question with a weak answer?"[15] Or to use a different cultural discourse, this is what the British Romantic poet John Keats famously defined as "Negative Capability" in great people and in great literature, and which, as he said, "Shakespeare possessed so enormously—I mean Negative Capability, that is, when a man is capable of being in uncertainties, mysteries, doubts, without any irritable reaching after fact and reason."[16]

So I am engaged here in explorative, tentative commentary more than in prosecuting a classical expository argument in a rigorous way. Sometimes the only way to fathom allusive texts in the end is in an allusive way, a poetic way. Those who love and study great literature know, like Keats, that it often can't be completely elucidated; things are hinted at and not always grasped in linear or clear cognitive ways. Or as Robert Frost famously put it, "Poetry is what is lost in translation." The same is true of the great religious texts which engage the mysteries of existence. And much classical Jewish textual commentary is in the form of gloss, word-by-word marginal commentary, with questions and answers flying back and forth between generations of commentators along the sides of the page; it is not written in the form of a treatise. So in a sense I am partly entering into that style as a way of enacting the texts' own rhetorical dynamic and the way in which they teach us to read them. I write here differently from the way one would write an article for a specialized academic journal—i.e., presenting my thesis, the evidence, what many other scholars have said, a critique of their arguments, my steps, and conclusions.

I must also note here that recent academic research in rabbinics views Talmudic stories as constructions of much later editors who compiled and embellished earlier traditions.[17] These scholars are skeptical about the extent to which the words attributed to the Talmudic Sages were actually spoken by them. My analyses are different from theirs, for my concern here is not in verifying the stories' historical authenticity, or discerning their various compositional strata, or entering that particular academic discourse. My interest lies in how they serve as teaching texts, models for reflection and repair of the teacher/student relation in Jewish tradition and contemporary culture. For the stories enact an idea of pedagogy in their very rhetorical construction. I would even venture to say that Talmudic texts are written to teach us as much about the process of teaching and learning as to fulfill any other goal. So I analyze the stories as they have been handed down in their final forms. I am interested in their inner aesthetic qualities as well as in their theological "afterlife"—to use the memorable phrase of the literary critic Walter Benjamin—that is, how the stories live past their original historical moment into later generations.[18]

There is another reason I have decided to focus this book primarily on an analysis of *stories* (as I did in giving the lectures which formed its basis), rather than on other kinds of material about teacher/student relations in Jewish tradition. My many years of teaching experience have led me to conclude that the most deeply received and absorbed teaching happens indirectly. Paul Tillich is often quoted as describing what goes wrong in pedagogy: "Our tendency as teachers is to throw answers like rocks at the heads of those who have not yet asked the questions."[19]

Unlike the rock-answers hurled at students' heads, good stories (and good teachers) arouse and instruct their hearers through subtly "enclothing" their meanings, to use R. Nahman of Bratslav's term, the great Hasidic leader, teacher, and story-teller of the nineteenth century. The desire to know is aroused through a lack, or glimpse of a trace which tracks a glimmering light to which one seeks attachment. The secret of stories, R. Nahman writes, is that they help people to awaken who have "fallen asleep," who are sunk in an existential darkness and lack of awareness. Stories, as he puts it, help people to "find their face" without the light overwhelming and blinding them. They "garb" and "enclothe" the light so it can be received; they enable the sleeper to awaken gently, like a blind person healing and slowly coming to see illumination. The story, he continues, is "clothing" for the face, so that the light of knowledge will not blind the person who is so sunk into darkness. Through the story, he or she can gradually awaken and see. The metaphor of "enclothing" is also a kind of alternative epistemology that avoids the traditional subject/object dualisms of Western philosophy. A garment both reveals and conceals its wearer and determines how a person presents her- or himself to others. Though there is no essential connection between the wearer and the garment, it still reveals something of the inner depth of the wearer, though the garment and wearer remain two separate entities. Being enclothed in a garment is also "uniting with" it on an intimate level and being "encompassed."[20]

My interest here, like R. Nahman's, finally lies in the existential meanings to be gleaned from these stories.[21] I read and write as a university teacher in the twenty-first century, concerned with larger issues of knowledge, spirituality, and education in our time, and also as an observant Jew. So this is *my* version of R. Eliezer ben Hyrcanus and his colleagues. This is also a book mainly intended for a broad general audience: Jews, non-Jews, readers of many different backgrounds, including advanced students of Jewish texts. It is for all those interested in educational issues and religious traditions; and especially for those seeking to be inspired and renewed in their teaching and learning. I hope each reader will find his or her own path through these pages. Some may delight in the drama of the stories and literary analyses; others in the theological speculations; others in the classical rabbinic exegeses; others in analyses of the personal vicissitudes of teacher/student relations; others in working their way through some of the denser endnotes.

Unlike in my previous books, I have chosen not to employ many technical terms from my academic field of literary theory, nor become embroiled here in its ideological and philosophical debates. And also unlike those works, I have not written this one for the postmodern academic looking for a theoretical discussion or ideological critique of Jewish texts.[22] This is a different kind of endeavor. My voice here is more personal; I position myself less as an objective critic standing above and outside these texts than as someone involved with them from the inside. Sometimes, also, the only way to deeply understand a text is to perform it, especially when dealing with allusive stories from the Oral Torah.[23] When trying to fashion a new way of writing and thinking about Jewish texts and education for his own time, Franz Rosenzweig, whom I cited at the beginning of this introduction, wrote:

> All criticism follows upon performance. The drama critic will have little to say, *before* it, no matter how clever he may be, for his criticism is not supposed to testify to what cleverness he had prior to the performance but to that which the performance evokes in him. Similarly, a theory of knowledge that precedes knowledge has no meaning. For all knowing—whenever anything is really known—is a unique act, and has its own method.[24]

In sum, I share here what these texts evoked in me, and my method is eclectic. In a scene we'll examine at length in chapter 3, R. Eliezer ben Hyrcanus on his death bed laments: "Much Torah have I learned, but I did not even skim from my teachers as much as a dog licks from the sea. Much Torah have I taught, but my disciples only drew from me as much as a painting stick from its tube." R. Joseph B. Soloveitchik writes of R. Eliezer's lament:

> Much more than what is written is what is not written; and around each written letter of the Torah, there is much that is not able to be written. The surrounding white space symbolizes the entire Oral Torah that is not able to be written.[25]

The laws about how the physical Torah scroll must be written enact this relation, R. Soloveitchik adds: the letters must not be allowed to touch each other and all the letters need to be surrounded by white space (*Menahot* 29b-30a). So many years, so much research, so much study went into the writing of this book. But so much of what I have learned and want to say remains unwritten. It can't be put between these covers. So much had to be edited out of the final manuscript; so much about the subject, I could not even explore. Above all, there are so many endless depths to these profound texts that I have not yet fathomed.

The Talmud also warns, "No one can understand the words of Torah until he has first stumbled in them" (*Gittin* 43a). I have stumbled many times trying to understand the material in the next chapters. The greatest stumbling block is that these rabbinic teachings are Oral Torah and not meant to be read about, but to be encountered in a live, face-to-face meeting between teacher and student, study partner and study partner, friend and friend. They should be voiced aloud in the original Hebrew, argued over, questioned. That encounter should give birth to unpredictable new insights, but also to pleasure, laughter, and intimacy.

Despite these limitations, I invite the reader of this book to be my *havruta*, my study partner, and consider my interpretations as a provisional starting point. Question me, argue with me, delight with me. Let us create our own relation to these stories. In other words, I invite you to "make yourself a teacher." Writing in an impersonal, detached, expository way about them is like presenting someone with the notes of a musical score to read, without ever performing or hearing it live. On the other hand, R. Nahman of Bratslav also once said: "He who is able to write a book and does not write it, is as one who has lost a child."[26] This book is my attempt to give birth in that ongoing chain of teachers and students.

• 1 •

"TORAH OF THE BELLY"

RABBI ELIEZER STARVES FOR A TEACHER

In the Talmudic definition, a teacher is not someone who has students,
but someone who has had a teacher.
—R. Léon Askénazi, "Morale et sainteté"

Drink water from your cistern [*bor*] and running waters from your
well [*be'er*]. Your springs [*ma'ayanot*] will gush forth, in streams in the
public squares.
—Proverbs 5:15–16

Toratekha be-tokh me'ai (Your teaching is in my innards).
—Psalms 40:9

Incline your ear and listen to the words of the Sages,
Pay attention to my wisdom.
It is good that you store them in your stomach.
—Proverbs 22:18

L ET'S set the stage with a gripping Talmudic tale of R. Eliezer's own
great teacher, R. Yohanan ben Zakkai, and his daring escape from a
besieged, blockaded, famine-stricken Jerusalem during the Jews' "Great
Revolt" against Rome in 66–73 CE. R. Eliezer is an accomplice in this dangerous act, along with his fellow student R. Yehoshua. R. Yohanan ben
Zakkai and the rabbinic leadership are unable to persuade the Zealots, the
radical Jewish rebel forces, to allow peace negotiations with the Romans.
The rebels have closed all exits from the city, forbidding escape. In a fur-

ther act of extremism, they burn all the food the city's wealthy citizens have donated and warehoused for the siege. Now the people will have no alternative but to side with them and fight the Romans. R. Yohanan secretly consults with his nephew Abba Sikra, a leader of the Zealots, who advises R. Yohanan of a strategy. Here is the famous story from the Talmudic tractate *Gittin* 55b-56b:

> The *biryoni* [Zealots] were then in the city. The Rabbis said to them: "Let us go out and make peace with them [the Romans]."
>
> They would not allow it, but on the contrary said, "Let us go out and fight them!"
>
> The Rabbis said: "You will not succeed."
>
> The Zealots then rose up and burnt the stores of wheat and barley so that a famine ensued. . . . Abba Sikra, the head of the *biryoni* in Jerusalem was the son of the sister of Rabban Yohanan ben Zakkai. [The latter] sent to him saying, "Come visit me in secret." When he came, he said to him [his nephew]: "How long are you going to carry on this way and kill all the people with starvation?"
>
> He replied: "What can I do? If I say a word to them, they will kill me."
>
> He said: "Devise some plan for me to escape. Perhaps I shall be able to save a little."
>
> He said to him: "Pretend to be deathly ill, and let everyone come to inquire about you. Bring something evil smelling and place it next to you so that they will say you are dead. Then have your disciples get under your bier, but no others, so that they shall not notice that you are still light; since they know that a living being is lighter than a corpse."
>
> R. Yohanan did so, and R. Eliezer went under the bier from one side and R. Yehoshua from the other. When they reached the city gate, some guards wanted to put a lance through the bier.
>
> He [Abba Sikra] said to them: "Shall [the Romans] say. 'They have pierced their Master?'"
>
> They wanted to give it a push. He said to them: "Shall they say that they pushed their Master?"
>
> They opened the city gate for him and he got out.[1]

The Jewish Zealot guards fear a trick but Abba Sikra artfully dissuades them from piercing the body to confirm R. Yohanan's death. They will embarrass themselves, he argues, before the watching Roman forces below if they perform such an act on the body of the great Rabbi and leader; it would show panic and loss of their control of the city. The guards then allow the false bier out of the city. R. Yohanan is carried out, comes to the camp of the Roman general Vespasian who is besieging the city, and correctly foretells that Vespasian will become the next Caesar. Vespasian, impressed with R. Yohanan, says: "You can make one request of me and I will grant it." Responds R. Yohanan: "Give me Yavneh and its Sages." In other words, do not destroy that coastal city and its scholars; allow me to go and save something there. R. Yohanan's request is granted. R. Eliezer and R. Yehoshua follow him to Yavneh where he reestablishes the rabbinic court and academy. They, in turn, become the leaders of the next generation.

The Temple and Jerusalem are destroyed in 70 CE, and the nation laid waste by the Romans. Massive numbers of Jews are killed and enslaved in the years of the Great Revolt against Rome, hundreds of cities and villages destroyed. But R. Yohanan was able to save far more than "a little"; he and his students' escape to Yavneh made it possible for the Jewish people to survive that catastrophe—and many succeeding periods of exile, war, and destruction. In Yavneh, the Sages creatively re-adapted the Torah to the needs of their time, gathered the oral traditions, and laid the foundations of rabbinic Judaism. Like R. Yohanan in the story, the Jewish people "seemed" to die, but returned to life. It would be another two thousand years until Jews would regain political independence in the Land of Israel with the reestablishment of the modern State in 1948. The three stories about R. Eliezer I'll examine in this book deal with the same themes as this tale of R. Yohanan's escape: political and familial conflicts, daring survival strategies, painful experiences of famine and exile, intimate relations between teachers and students, and spiritual assertion in the face of death.

As a major figure in the foundations of rabbinic Judaism, R. Eliezer appears not only in many stories in rabbinic literature, but is often cited as a major source of legal opinion, from the very first pages of the Mishnah and Talmud, onwards. Later generations referred to him as R. Eliezer *ha-Gadol,* "the Great," and the leading teachers of the next generation were his students. R. Yehoshua is said to have praised R. Eliezer by kissing the stone reserved for R. Eliezer to sit on while he taught, saying: "The stone is like Mount Sinai and he who sat upon it is like the Ark of the Covenant." (*Song of Songs Rabbah,* I.3:1–2). But rabbinic sources often also portray R. Eliezer as an overwhelming, adamant, and even lonely personality. The conflicts between innovation and preservation involved in the remaking of Judaism at Yavneh and R. Eliezer's role in it, also led to tragic personal consequences. In the famous story of his dispute with the Sages, including R. Yehoshua, over "The Oven of Akhnai" (*Bava Metzi'a* 59b), R. Eliezer's obstinacy in the face of the majority with whom he disagreed led to his ostracism (*niddui*). In his poignant death scene in *Sanhedrin* 68a-b, the Talmud describes how he "put his two arms over his heart and bewailed them," saying:

> Woe to you, two arms of mine that are like two Scrolls of the Law being rolled up. Much Torah I learned, and much Torah I taught. Much Torah I learned, but I did not even skim from my teachers as much as a dog licks from the sea. Much Torah I taught, but my disciples only drew from me as much as a painting stick from its tube.

We'll look at these three stories about R. Eliezer in light of each other: the tale of his beginnings as a student, the fierce dispute with his colleagues over the oven of Akhnai, and his lonely passing. Though these stories are scattered in different places in the Talmud and Midrash, the traditional student of the Torah would easily sense their "intertextuality." Like the Talmud's editors, the traditional learner would have the whole corpus simultaneously in mind, always reading it "backwards and forwards." From a literary point of view as well, the three stories are also beautifully interwoven in theme, structure, and image. They are not only *about* teachers and students; they also enact a *way of teaching* through their dramatic literary and rhetorical structures, their images, metaphors, allusions, enigmas. They have no simple moral, nor can they be reduced to any concise expository statements about pedagogy. In that sense, they are not didactic, but they are deep and self-conscious teachings. They beckon and seduce us to enter their world, to sit among the Sages and be their students, to argue with them, to feel their exaltation and pain, to judge, and to question our judgments.

"HUNGER IS THE BEST SEASONING."—OLD LATIN PROVERB

Let's now take a step back to a rabbinic story that tells how this famous Sage, R. Eliezer, found the path that enabled him to become who he was. How did it all start? What kind of a student was this man who became such a leader in Israel? What moved him? How did his relation to R. Yohanan begin and progress? The path was not at all what one might expect. But the story we are about to read is embryonic of his entire character and future life. For all its seeming simplicity, it is nuanced, artfully constructed, and will require close attention.

We'll first read it as a whole, then go back to it piece by piece, circling around scenes, lines, and phrases again and again to elicit meanings. In other words, we'll read it like a literary critic reads a poem, a psychologist interprets a dream, and classical Jewish study partners (*hevrutot*) study a sacred text together.

What were the beginnings of Rabbi Eliezer ben Hyrcanus?

He was twenty-two years old and had not studied Torah. One time he resolved: "I will go and study Torah with Rabban Yohanan ben Zak-kai."

Said his father Hyrcanus to him: "Not a taste of food shall you get before you have ploughed the entire furrow." He rose early in the morning, ploughed the entire furrow, and then left for Jerusalem.

It is told: That day was the eve of the Sabbath, and he went for the Sabbath meal to his father-in-law's. And some say: He tasted nothing from six hours before the eve of the Sabbath until six hours after the departure of the Sabbath.

As he was walking along the road he saw a stone. He picked it up and put it in his mouth. And some say: It was cattle dung.

He went to spend the night at a hostel.

Then he went and sat before Rabban Yohanan ben Zakkai in Jeru-salem—until a bad breath rose from his mouth. Said Rabban Yohanan ben Zakkai to him:

"Eliezer, my son, have you eaten at all today?" Silence.

Rabban Yohanan ben Zakkai asked him again.

Again silence.

Rabban Yohanan ben Zakkai sent for the owners of his hostel and asked them: "Did Eliezer have anything at all to eat in your place?"

"No," they said, "We thought he was very likely eating with you, Master."

He said to them: "And I thought he was likely eating with you! You and I, between us, left Rabbi Eliezer to perish!"

Then Rabban Yohanan said to him: "Even as bad breath rose from your mouth, so shall your fame travel for your mastery of Torah."

When Hyrcanus, his father, heard he was studying Torah with Rabban Yohanan ben Zakkai, he declared: "I shall go and ban my son Eliezer from my possessions!"

It is told: That day Rabban Yohanan ben Zakkai sat expounding in Jerusalem and all the great ones of Israel sat before him. When he heard that Hyrcanus was coming, he appointed guards and said to them, "If Hyrcanus comes, do not let him sit down."

Hyrcanus arrived and they would not let him sit. But he pushed on ahead until he reached the place near Ben Tzitzit ha-Kasat, Nakdimon ben Guryon, and Ben Kalba Savu'a. He sat among them, trembling.

On that day, Rabban Yohanan ben Zakkai fixed his gaze upon Eliezer and said to him: "Open, deliver the exposition."

"I am unable to open, unable to speak." Rabbi Eliezer pleaded.

Rabban Yohanan pressed him to do it, and the disciples pressed him. He stood up, opened, and delivered a discourse about matters which no ear had ever heard. As the words came from his mouth, Rabban Yohanan ben Zakkai stood up, kissed him upon his head and exclaimed, "Rabbi Eliezer, Master, you have taught me the truth!"

Before the time had come to recess, Hyrcanus, his father, stood up and declared: "My Masters, I came here only in order to ban my son Eliezer from my possessions. Now, all my possessions shall be given to Eliezer my son. All his brothers are disinherited and will have nothing of them." (*Avot de-Rabbi Natan (A)*, ch. 6)[2]

This story of R. Eliezer's beginnings reads like a dream text, filled with compressed intense images, unanswered questions, powerful tensions and desires. From whence comes his desire to learn Torah? Why does he not eat? Why does he not even reveal his hunger to R. Yohanan or anyone else? Why is it so hard for him to "open" and speak? I have puzzled over this story endlessly, read many commentaries, entertained many answers to these questions. I present some below. But there is something so primal, so multilayered about the story, its plot, characters, dialogues, and images that—like all profound literature—it finally exceeds rational explanations and commentary. The questions the story raises seem more penetrating and alive than the answers. Perhaps this is also because Oral Torah can't just be read; its structure defers meaning and makes us perform it, actively engage it, add to it, question it further, study it over and over. Like R. Eliezer, the story does not break its silences so easily.

On one level R. Eliezer's painful flight from home to find his "spiritual father and family" is about a student's initiation and transformation into a teacher. The narrative is rhetorically designed around contrasts such as hunger/fullness; isolation/community; self-alienation/identity; passivity/activity; Written Torah/Oral Torah; earth/heaven; conservatism/innovation. Before probing the story further, let's step back again for a moment for some other clues and view R. Eliezer from the perspective of the teacher, R. Yohanan, to whom he runs and for whom he gives up everything. Rabbinic tradition ascribes to R. Yohanan the following famous passage in the mishnaic tractate *Pirkei Avot*, the "Ethics of the Fathers."

> R. Yohanan ben Zakkai had the following five disciples: R. Eliezer ben Hyrcanus, R. Yehoshua ben Hananiah, R. Yose ha-Kohen, R. Shimon ben Nathaniel, and R. Eleazar ben Arakh.
>
> He used to recount their praises: "Eliezer ben Hyrcanus is a plastered cistern, which does not lose not a drop. Yehoshua ben Hananiah—happy is she who bore him. Yose is pious. Shimon ben Nathaniel is a fearer of sin, Eleazar ben Arakh is a welling spring.
>
> He used to say: "If all the Sages of Israel were in a scale of the balance, and Eliezer ben Hyrcanus on the other side, he would outweigh them all."
>
> Abba Shaul, however, said in his name: "If all the Sages of Israel were in a scale of the balance and Eliezer ben Hyrcanus with them, and Eleazar ben Arakh on the other side, he would outweigh them all."
> (*Pirkei Avot* 2:8)

In this listing of "multiple intelligences," why does R. Eliezer ben Hyrcanus "outweigh" or "balance" the others? What is the meaning of the metaphor of the scale? And which trait is most important for a culture? Is it the *bor sud* (plastered cistern)—the student or teacher who can preserve, contain, and keep a people rooted to its history and the sources of its being? Or, as in Abba Shaul's version, is it the *ma'ayan ha-mitgabber*, the "overflowing spring"—the capacity to keep a culture alive by innovation and inspiration? If we had to choose which force is most needed in any given historical moment, how would we decide? What is the proper balance between the two? And at times of great turmoil and destruction—whether in an individual's life, or the life of a nation—which is most important?

The cistern and the overflowing spring are also fertile metaphors for the teacher/student relation and for ways of receiving and transmitting knowledge. A plastered cistern is a large, deep, hewn-stone container storing precious rainwater, preserving it for times of need. In the arid Middle Eastern landscape, this is a matter of life and death. This type of student or teacher is a vessel, with immense powers to absorb knowledge from the outside, be faithful to his or her teacher, guard a tradition, and never forget anything. The welling spring, by contrast, feeds from its own underground streams, ever renewed and fresh as it gushes forth to give life. That kind of student or teacher draws from hidden inner resources and restlessly overflows with creative new insights.[3]

Both cistern and wellspring channel sources of life, but in different ways. The size of the cistern determines the volume of water held. But the wellspring connects to an ongoing flow, unstoppable and measureless. Using kabbalistic-Hasidic terminology, we might say that the one represents the *mekabbel* (the receiver) and the other the *mashpia* (the giver)—or, the *or* (light) and *keli* (vessel). The oscillation between the two is the dynamic of any living relationship. The vessel, in many ways, must be stronger than what it holds, lest the contents scatter, diffuse, and disappear.

Bor is the word in Hebrew for "cistern"; *be'er* for "well"; *ma'ayan* for "wellspring." All three terms are used in the epigraph to this chapter from Proverbs 5:15–16. *Bor* and *be'er* sound quite similar: just one letter makes the difference. What changes a "cistern" into a more open "well," or into an even more flowing "wellspring"? What is the interplay between these different forms of closure, openness, and flow in the teacher/student relation and within a student her- or himself? Says R. Eliezer in a famous statement in *Sukkah* 28a: "I never said anything I did not hear from my teacher." But in the story of his beginnings, we are told that "He stood up, opened, and delivered a discourse about matters which no ear had ever heard. As the words came from his mouth, Rabban Yohanan ben Zakkai stood up, kissed him upon his head and exclaimed, 'Rabbi Eliezer, Master, you have taught me the truth!'"[4]

An interesting choice of words. "You have taught me *the truth.*" Didn't R. Yohanan know the truth before? What kind of truth did he learn from R. Eliezer? And what might be the dangers of such an intense "absolute" truth?—an issue we will take up in chapter 2. For the moment, we know that both the plastered cistern and the overflowing spring can be overwhelming forces. A cistern's waters can also deteriorate by being stagnant; a wellspring's can lose force through dispersion or by overflowing the vessel meant to receive them. In the scale metaphor, when one side of a scale "outweighs" the other, it also forces the other side down. In other words, R. Yohanan's description of R. Eliezer's "outweighing them all" might also hint at a possible dangerous excess and a need to balance the strong tendencies of the *bor sud*, the "plastered cistern," with a counterweight.

This seminal story of R. Eliezer's beginnings also involves balancing problems in the relations between parents and children, teachers and students in Jewish tradition—and in everyday life. To what extent is the teacher's role complementary to, or in tension with, the parent's?[5] Whether we desire it or not, consciously or unconsciously, parents are our teachers in profound ways. We absorb formal and informal teachings from them almost against our will, simply by living with them. Later in life, and despite ourselves, we often repeat their behaviors. The areas of overlap between parents and teachers are delicate and dangerous. There are biological parents and spiritual parents. Teachings of parents occur not just through words, but in silence, through smell, touch, rhythm. In our story R. Eliezer, however, does not have a father who is willing or able to teach him Torah. From the very opening lines, the tension between father and son is strong. R. Eliezer is an outsider in his family.

Now, we can circle back, "begin again," and read the story more carefully and slowly. Below, I divide the story into its dramatic scenes and give them titles to facilitate closer analysis and illuminate the artful construction of the narrative.

Scene 1: Fathers and Sons

> What were the beginnings of Rabbi Eliezer ben Hyrcanus?
> He was twenty-two years old and had not studied Torah. One time he resolved: "I will go and study Torah with Rabban Yohanan ben Zakkai."
> Said his father Hyrcanus to him, "Not a taste of food shall you get before you have ploughed the entire furrow." He rose early in the morning, ploughed the entire furrow, and then left for Jerusalem.

In this version of the story from *Avot de-Rabbi Natan,* R. Eliezer is an adult who is ignorant of all Torah learning, an *am ha-aretz* in all senses of the word. *Am ha-aretz* is a rabbinic term literally meaning "people of the land," but pejoratively signifying common people ignorant of the Torah. He has to spend his youth plowing the fields of his father. Later, R. Eliezer will toil in the other "fields of Torah study" of his spiritual father, R. Yohanan. The "stony furrows" are like the spiritually inhospitable environment of his biological family, from which his yearning and aspiration separate him. Hyrcanus is a gruff father, all business, and insensitive to his son's very different "hungers." Eliezer desires not the physical food his father threatens to withhold; he seeks another kind of nourishment to fill an inner ache. This is a story, of course, of so many fathers and sons.

It is told: That day was the eve of the Sabbath, and he went for the Sabbath meal to his father-in-law's. And some say: He tasted nothing from six hours before the eve of the Sabbath until six hours after the departure of the Sabbath.

As he was walking along the road he saw a stone; he picked it up and put it in his mouth. And some say: it was cattle dung.

He went to spend the night at a hostel.

Then he went and sat before Rabban Yohanan ben Zakkai in Jerusalem—until a bad breath rose from his mouth. Said Rabban Yohanan ben Zakkai to him:

"Eliezer, my son, have you eaten at all today?" Silence.

Rabban Yohanan ben Zakkai asked him again.

Again silence.

Rabban Yohanan ben Zakkai sent for the owners of his hostel and asked them: "Did Eliezer have anything at all to eat in your place?"

"No," they said, "We thought "he was very likely eating with you Master."

He said to them: "And I thought he was very likely eating with you! You and I, between us, left Rabbi Eliezer to perish!"

Even after Eliezer runs away to Jerusalem, he remains isolated—both at his lodgings and among the family of his "spiritual father" R. Yohanan ben Zakkai. He is not "fed" by anyone. His hunger is not recognized until it becomes intolerable to the others as well. In the two stories we will discuss later, R. Eliezer will undergo other traumatic separations from his colleagues and students. The first, when he is banned after a critical dispute in the rabbinic academy; the second on his death bed when he reencounters those who caused him such pain. In his final words, he speaks again of his hunger and thirst: he could only take from his teachers, what "a dog could lick from the sea." This is a hunger for something as broad and restlessly alive as the sea, far beyond the capacity of any "cistern" to contain. Or as the biblical book of Ecclesiastes famously puts it, "All the rivers run into the sea, but the sea is not full" (1:7).

The theme of hunger runs throughout all our stories, from the famine and starvation of the besieged city of Jerusalem and the burning of its provisions by the Jewish rebels in a suicidal political act to R. Eliezer's physical and spiritual hungers from his early years to his end. In the story of his origins R. Eliezer is condemned to literal hunger by his biological father, but he is not in need of actual food. When he finds his spiritual father, he thinks he is being fed, but his teacher reminds him that he must sustain his body too. He learns to accept both physical and spiritual nourishment.[6] Body and soul also need to be balanced.

Scene 2: "The Hunger Artist": Why Doesn't R. Eliezer Eat?

Like Kafka's story "The Hunger Artist," this Talmudic tale is luminous and enigmatic. Walter Benjamin once described Kafka's stories as "fairy tales for dialecticians."[7] Talmudic stories can often have that feeling as well. Or to use Erich Auerbach's elegant description of biblical narrative, this story of R. Eliezer's beginnings is "fraught with background."[8] The provocative enigmas of biblical and Talmudic literature should not be simplified, smoothed over, or abstracted. Through their "fraught background," they hint and beckon their students beyond—where the infinite is touched in the tangled knot of relations between God and humanity. The stories often conceal as much as they reveal.

So I prefer to avoid (and reject) a one-dimensional oedipal reading of the story as a "rebellion against the father." Rachel Adelman has shrewdly observed in her commentary on this narrative that there are three levels to the father/son drama here: (1) biological father and son [Hyrcanus and Eliezer]; (2) intellectual father and son [R. Yohanan and Eliezer]; and (3) the ultimate Father—God, Moses, Sinai—and those who receive the Torah represented by R. Eliezer. In the story's world of Torah learning, "the oedipal drama is undermined," Adelman writes, "for it is specifically the father figure, R. Yohanan, who encourages this surpassing."[9] That is, he is the one who enables R. Eliezer to speak, kisses and confirms him, saying "Master, you have taught me the truth."

R. Eliezer's hunger, like so many of our deepest desires, grips the entire self; such desires are another kind of forceful "wellspring" that thrust up from a place we do not know. From the very beginning, his yearnings are raw and, as it were, "unspeakable" in his father's house. His intensity, his passions, his suffering to learn Torah and find his teacher—his isolation and his exaltation—interweave spiritual and physical desire. The story speaks also about the harder paths that those who come to learn and love Torah must endure: Is R. Eliezer perhaps exploring his own capacity for self-abnegation? Like so many seekers, R. Eliezer has a deep hunger for something more, though he is barely able to articulate it and is not understood by others. Feeling that ache is surely part of the eros of knowledge, an idea I will return to in a few pages. Intense physical hunger keeps a person awake; it takes over one's consciousness, makes its imperious demands. R. Eliezer wants to eat only from *the* special tree of wisdom and not any other; he will be satisfied only by going to the sacred center of Jerusalem and studying there with the greatest teacher.

Let us imagine him, then, walking on his way alone and hungry. He puts inedible matter into his mouth: earth, stones—the stuff of his previous aborted life of plowing and tilling soil. We could suppose that he simply did not have any money—or that he chose not to take money with him when he ran away from his father's house to make a clean break. But neither does he later request any help from fellow students, his hosts, or his teacher in Jerusalem.

Food, of course, symbolically mediates all kinds of relationships, maternal nourishment as well as power struggles between parents and children. Sharing food also forms identity and community, it turns "nature" into "culture." Cooking is a kind of magic really, but also a type of dialogue with the material world. In eating and integrating the world outside, the body also carries on an inner process of discernment; it distinguishes between what is good and what is indigestible excess. So eating transforms the outside into the inside and represents "internalization," "inner knowing." Or to use the felicitous expression of R. Askénazi, "Food is the world transformed into a person." We transform the food and it transforms us (and that's also what true learning should accomplish). If we do not eat, we eventually lose consciousness and life.

Food also reminds us of the precariousness of our existence and that we are not the origin of our being. The need to constantly nourish and sustain ourselves reminds us of our finitude in a way no abstract philosophy can. By making us acutely aware of being created, as R. Askénazi also notes, it can be a powerful vehicle of religious awareness. One must eat to live, and so the presence of the highest values depends, in the end, on the fact of physical nourishment—a kind of philosophical scandal and true mystery. It's no wonder, then, that the meal is so often the basis of rites of faith; it is a "liturgy of the creature recognizing him or her as such."[10] Each gesture of life returns to nourishment of the soul and heart as well as the body.

Eating, in sum, can surpass the ability of the intellect to convey cultural or spiritual messages. A sure way to change one's consciousness is by changing one's menu, as most spiritual traditions well understand. Some nourishment, though, comes to us easily and with pleasure—milk from a mother's breasts or water from flowing streams. Some comes only through arduous labor, like the sowing, plowing, reaping, grinding, and baking necessary for bread. So it is not fortuitous that bread, milk, wine, and water represent different kinds of knowing and learning in classical Jewish sources. Some knowledge flows to us like waters from heaven or from underground streams—as in prophetic or other revelatory modes. Some comes through "suckling"; as the Talmud famously says: "Why are the words of Torah compared to a breast? As with the breast, each time the child touches it, he finds milk in it, so it is with the words of Torah. Each time a person reasons in them, he finds pleasure in them" *Eruvin* 54b).[11] Other kinds of knowledge come only through struggle and a long period of "digestion."

And each of these modes involves a different kind of teacher/student relationship. When R. Eliezer's foremost student, R. Akiva, is jailed by the Romans and sentenced to death for teaching Torah, R. Akiva's own great disciple, R. Shimon bar Yohai, comes to him and asks to be taught Torah. "More than the calf wants to suck, the cow wants to suckle," answers R. Akiva (*Pesahim* 112a). This female suckling metaphor involves a special kind of reciprocal binding and flow. The desire of the infant to nurse activates the fresh milk of the mother, just as the desire of the student to learn activates the desire of the teacher to teach. The cow needs the calf to suck and draw forth its milk; the mother needs the child to nurse or her breasts will ache. Who indeed then controls the relationship—mother or child, student or teacher? Who gives identity to the other?[12]

For R. Eliezer, the physical food comes hard, from plowing and struggle with the earth, and his spiritual food will also come hard. He puts a stone in his mouth, sucks it almost like the baby whose oral desires are so strong, but who does not yet know how to distinguish between objects. The English word "infant" indeed comes from a Latin root meaning "unable to speak/no speech" and R. Eliezer himself is without speech for most of the narrative. He is placed in a stereotypical feminized position through much of the story, subject to others, without voice and power.

Or perhaps R. Eliezer is cleansing himself of the "food" he has been eating in his father's home to make room for the "spiritual food" he will ingest in the school of his spiritual father, R. Yohanan ben Zakkai. And "not eating" is a kind of symbolic death that R. Eliezer needs to undergo in his transformation from *am ha-aretz*, ignorant man of the land, to teacher of heavenly mysteries. Later, he will endure a "symbolic death" when banned by his colleagues and lament his inability to pass on all he had learned. In all three stories, he is in a space between worlds and identities, subject to being sucked empty. R. Yohanan ben Zakkai described him as a "plastered cistern." Perhaps not eating is hollowing himself out further, opening himself up to make a receptacle for what he desires to learn. That, too, is a way growth occurs—through a necessary dissolution of the previous stage, followed by a period of emptiness which makes a "space" for something new to enter. The cistern has first to be dug out of the earth; its emptiness and hardness are requisite qualities for its purpose as container.[13] In hollowing himself out, he could be preparing to "give birth" to a new self, which will also give birth to new Torah.

"Stones," "earth," and "dirt" seem to be the most common and worthless things—all that R. Eliezer was running away from when he was plowing. Now they are elements he must transform as the *am ha-aretz*; the ignorant man of the earth becomes a scholar of Torah. They are also the most elemental materials from which sustaining food grows. They endure beyond human life. This is the Torah R. Eliezer is seeking, a Torah which is both the root of his life and the highest wisdom, as eternal as the everlasting rocks and hills. This is the Torah for which he will live his life and which he will adamantly defend as a "plastered cistern," even when it causes him great personal pain and isolation.

Melila Hellner-Eshed, a specialist in both Jewish pedagogy and Jewish mysticism, suggests another way to understand R. Eliezer's abstinence. There are a few basic reasons why we do not eat: (1) inability to purchase food; (2) ascetic tendencies; (3) or when we are so full or engaged that we forget, or do not want, to eat. R. Eliezer, she thinks, could be the third case. He yearns to be filled with Torah and upon finding his teacher, R. Yohanan ben Zakkai, he begins to be filled with that for which he has given up everything else; and so he no longer connects to the realm of ordinary eating.

Other stories indeed portray him as an extreme type with a very intense personality.[14] The plastered cistern metaphor also signifies this ability to intensely compress; the kind of person who has powers of great concentration, of "holding in," becomes a large vessel for the tradition. But not eating can also be a sign of ill health, and R. Eliezer is indeed ill in a way, sick with longing, disoriented, alone.

Not only does R. Eliezer refrain from eating, he also refrains from speaking, even after his breakaway from home and finding his teacher. Why does he not answer R. Yohanan ben Zakkai's queries? A psychoanalytically inclined reader might argue that he feels "guilty" for leaving his father and so cannot eat; he is ambivalent, paralyzed. His father's last words were: "not a taste of food will you get before you have ploughed the entire furrow." Perhaps R. Eliezer has internalized those words: he will not eat until he has ploughed the entire furrow of Torah study.

Or perhaps, in good Talmudic fashion, one could interpret it the opposite way: because R. Eliezer is a "plastered cistern," he remains "faithful" to his father. He is silent out of that faithfulness. He does not want to reveal who he is, or why he has not eaten, since it would cause embarrassment to his father. It is only *after* R. Yohanan ben Zakkai learns how long R. Eliezer has withheld himself from eating that R. Yohanan exclaims how great a Torah scholar R. Eliezer will become. "Thereupon Rabban Yohanan said to him: 'Even as bad breath rose from your mouth, so shall your fame travel for your mastery of Torah.'" The ability to be faithful even under duress and to be a faithful transmitter of tradition is critical to becoming a great Torah Sage. As faithful as an unmovable stone.

Scene 3: Torah of the Mouth/Oral Torah

> When Hyrcanus, his father, heard that he was studying Torah with Rabban Yohanan ben Zakkai, he declared: "I shall go and ban my son Eliezer from my possessions."
>
> It is told: That day Rabban Yohanan ben Zakkai sat expounding in Jerusalem and all the great ones of Israel sat before him. When he heard that Hyrcanus was coming, he appointed guards and said to them, "If Hyrcanus comes, do not let him sit down."
>
> Hyrcanus arrived and they would not let him sit. But he pushed on ahead until he reached the place near Ben Tzitzit ha-Kasat, Nakdimon ben Guryon, and Ben Kalba Savu'a. He sat among them trembling.

On that day Rabban Yohanan ben Zakkai fixed his gaze upon Eliezer and said to him: "Open, deliver the exposition."

"I am unable to open, unable to speak." Rabbi Eliezer pleaded.

Rabban Yohanan pressed him to do it and the disciples pressed him. He stood up, opened, and delivered a discourse about matters which no ear had ever heard. As the words came from his mouth, Rabban Yohanan ben Zakkai stood up, kissed him upon his head and exclaimed, "Rabbi Eliezer, Master, you have taught me the truth!"

How does the cistern release its precious waters? What does it take for R. Yohanan to "open R. Eliezer's mouth" and deliver supernal words of Torah "no ear had ever heard" before all the notables, his colleagues, his teacher, and his father? How can the relationship between the physical father and son be healed after its radical rupture; and how can the relationship between the spiritual father and son also attain maturity? Interestingly, there is no direct verbal response from R. Eliezer in the story to anyone else's speech except at its conclusion, when he responds to R. Yohanan ben Zakkai's urging to "Open, deliver the exposition"—*Petah u-derash. Petah* means in Hebrew "to open," and in this context also "begin." The double meaning here is rich: open yourself and open up the Torah inside you, open its secrets. R. Eliezer responds, "I am unable to open."

In every other instance in the story when speech is addressed to him, he does not respond verbally. Neither to his father's initial warning, nor to R. Yohanan's questionings as to whether he has eaten, nor to R. Yohanan's prophecy/promise that he will become a great teacher of Torah. His very first words, "I will go and study Torah," seem to be part of an inner monologue or a displaced, belated announcement to his father who then reacts negatively. But father and son never enter into reciprocal dialogue.

So his mouth is closed on many levels—unable to eat, unable to speak. Perhaps this is a stage in all transformative learning—a stage of muteness, silence, emptiness, when one has to let go of previous knowledge and of many parts of oneself in order to absorb the new. In a famous Talmudic story, R. Ze'eira relates that upon ascending to the Land of Israel, he fasted for one hundred days in order to "forget" the dialectics of the Babylonian Talmud so that he then would be able to absorb the very different learning style of the Jerusalem Talmud (*Bava Metzi'a* 85a). That, too, might be a similar self-forgetting and self-silencing, a desire for new creation.

A withholding silence can also be very powerful, as the poet Adrienne Rich so eloquently writes in "Cartographies of Silence":

Silence can be a plan
rigorously executed

the blueprint of a life

It is a presence
it has a history a form

Do not confuse it
with any kind of absence.

So the silent R. Eliezer is now pressed on all sides, by his father, his hunger, his muteness, and then finally by R. Yohanan and the fellow students who "press him" until he opens. Then out flow words "never heard" before. From a realm beyond human speech, he now captures divine creative speech and recreates himself. The cistern has become a wellspring. Oral Torah is born. The mouth opens, which opens up the Torah as well. Still, the narrator only tells us *about* the words R. Eliezer speaks, but we do not actually hear them from R. Eliezer's mouth.

Though R. Eliezer is infantilized in many ways throughout the story, he now transforms, opens his mouth, and teaches his teacher. He is nourished, fed, and opened by R. Yohanan and his fellow students. This last part of the tale prompts us to ask: How do you open a student? The teacher needs to recognize the right moment and give the student the permission she or he needs. R. Yohanan authorizes R. Eliezer. But as R. Daniel Landes also points out, R. Yohanan is not just creating a student who "has knowledge" but is "opening him up to *derash.*" *Derash* means the independent, creative, innovative aspects of Torah interpretation.[15] *Derash* itself breaks open the text, penetrates to its hidden meanings, cracks open its surface. And here "teaching" is also a "breaking." It breaks open the student and perhaps the teacher too.

It is tempting to further interpret the web of gendered images surrounding R. Eliezer's character, but I would again resist any simplistic decoding of "empty vessels," "pressing," "giving birth," or "spurting forth" in the story. The learning of Torah is a love, a passionate love, involving all aspects of human personality. Behind this love and yearning for Torah is another love, hunger, and yearning for God. Melila Hellner-Eshed puts it eloquently in her discussion of the highly erotic metaphors in the *Zohar*, one of the foundational texts of the Jewish mystical tradition: "We must ask the question whether Torah study is a sublimation of sexual desire, or conversely, whether the ultimate or truest 'Eros' is between man and God through the Torah, of which the sexual act between man and woman is merely a symbol or echo."[16] Our story of R. Eliezer, in its multiple networks of overt and covert associations, contains many relationships that ache for connection and union: between father and son; sibling and sibling; friend and friend, lover and beloved; male "giver" and female "receiver"; birth-giving mother and suckling child.

At the story's end, the "receiver" becomes the "giver." The cistern becomes a wellspring. The Ga'on of Vilna, R. Eliyahu (1720–1797), one of the greatest Torah scholars of the past three hundred years (*Ga'on* meaning "Talmudic genius"), derives a developmental linear psychological process in the teacher/student relationship from the verses from Proverbs 5:15–16, which I cited in the epigraph to this chapter: "Drink water from your cistern [*bor*]; and running waters from your well [*be'er*]; your springs [*ma'ayanot*] will gush forth, in streams in the public square." The verse, in his view, is not simply employing a series of metaphorical synonyms for poetic effect. Classical rabbinic interpretation generally assumes no unnecessary repetition or simple rhetorical flourishes in Torah texts, but asks why each term is necessary and what it spiritually signifies. A person who drinks from a cistern, notes the Ga'on, has to work arduously: dig the cistern, journey to it each time, and then laboriously draw up the water. To drink from a *be'er* (which can also mean a "small spring") takes minimal effort, since it spurts forth at one's feet. *Ma'ayanot* are the even stronger springs that gush forth into the city squares, requiring no effort at all to reach or drink from. Such are the sequential stages of Torah learning the Ga'on interprets: the first (cistern) is when one begins and goes to one's teacher to study; one needs to apply great effort to gather and absorb knowledge. The second (spring) is when one can learn by oneself without a teacher and innovate independently. In the third (gushing, overflowing springs), one becomes a teacher to others, and one's teachings flow beyond into the public squares, even to those one has not personally taught. [17]

Scene 4: Finale

What prompts, though, the move from one stage to the next? How does one overcome the student's inhibitions? How does the teacher facilitate the transitions? In our story, R. Yohanan enables the passage from the second to the third stage by carefully orchestrating a scene to be performed in front of R. Eliezer's angry father, Hyrcanus. He "stages" exactly the right moment and setting to press R. Eliezer.

> When Hyrcanus, his father, heard he was studying Torah with Rabban Yohanan ben Zakkai, he declared: "I shall go and ban my son Eliezer from my possessions!"
>
> It is told: That day Rabban Yohanan ben Zakkai sat expounding in Jerusalem and all the great ones of Israel sat before him. When he heard that Hyrcanus was coming, he appointed guards and said to them, "If Hyrcanus comes, do not let him sit down."
>
> Hyrcanus arrived and they would not let him sit. But he pushed on ahead until he reached the place near Ben Tzitzit ha-Kasat, Nakdimon ben Guryon, and Ben Kalba Savu'a. He sat among them, trembling.

The father is trembling, and although the text does not overtly tell us, it hints that the son is also trembling. The three names mentioned here, Ben Tzitzit ha-Kasat, Nakdimon ben Guryon, and Ben Kalba Savu'a, are the same wealthy figures named in part of our famous Talmudic account of *Gittin* 55b-56b about the Roman siege of Jerusalem and the escape of R. Yohanan. They had supported the city with stores of food and firewood, and these storehouses the Zealots had burned, bringing the crisis to its bitter climax. That part of the Talmudic story relates:

> He [the Roman emperor] then sent against them Vespasian the Caesar who came and besieged Jerusalem for three years. There were in it three men of great wealth, Nakdimon ben Guryon, Ben Kalba Savu'a and Ben Tzitzit ha-Kasat . . . . One of these said to the people of Jerusalem, "I will keep them in wheat and barley." A second said, "I will keep them in wine, oil and salt." The third said, "I will keep them in wood." The Rabbis considered the offer of wood the most generous, since R. Hisda used to hand all his keys to his servant save that of the wood, for R. Hisda used to say, "A storehouse of wheat requires sixty stores

of wood [for fuel]." These men were in a position to keep the city for twenty-one years. (*Gittin* 56a) [18]

As Robert Eisen notes, the author of our story of R. Eliezer's origins takes pains to specifically name them again. Eisen suggests that "when Hyrcanus sits among them and trembles, it may be because he realizes that even the wealthy—those who best represent the material life he lives—are students of Torah."[19] But Hyrcanus may still simultaneously be trembling with anger, having come not only in wrath to disinherit his son, but also been denied a seat. Not deterred by anything, he pushes on ahead, neatly falling into the "trap" R. Yohanan has set. It seems that R. Yohanan also shrewdly knows how to "teach" and "open" a character like Hyrcanus.

But does the father then transform himself after hearing his son's supernal words of Torah?

> Before the time had come to recess, Hyrcanus, his father, stood up and declared: "My Masters, I came here only in order to ban my son Eliezer from my possessions. Now, all my possessions shall be given to Eliezer my son. All his brothers are disinherited and will have nothing of them."

Is this a validation, or is there something dissonant and unresolved here? Isn't R. Eliezer's father, Hyrcanus, accepting his son for the wrong reason—the public honor he is given? Instead of reuniting the family, his father now disinherits R. Eliezer's brothers in place of him. So his father is the same character he was at the beginning of the story. His vocabulary consists of threats and is only about material possessions. There is a certain tragedy, then, at the end. Is R. Eliezer ever healed? Or will he always retain some of that inner emptiness and the stoniness of the cistern? His father wanted to "ban" him, but relents at the last moment; his colleagues, as we will see in chapter 2, ban him not from material possessions but from his spiritual ones, undo his role as a teacher. They relent only when it is too late.

At its end, we also need to remember that R. Eliezer's story is told "retrospectively" by the composers and editors of rabbinic literature. They are linking themselves to him and him to us. The story is commenting on the power of Oral Torah itself and the power of those who are telling this story and passing it on to us. In other words, the story's editors and its faithful audience also know that this is *the* R. Eliezer who will become one of the greatest builders and teachers of the Oral Torah, the *Torah she-be-al peh—* literally, "the Torah of the Mouth."[20] So the transformation of R. Eliezer's breath from mute and sour to fluent and sweet transforms him into a living Torah. A Torah inscribed on the body and given face-to-face, person-to-person between teacher and disciple. As Moses is said to have received it from God and as each traditional student receives it from her or his teacher until today. R. Yohanan ben Zakkai will "kiss" R. Eliezer on the head after his *derashah*, call him "Master" to affirm his new status—a gesture of the mouth, of intimacy and confirmation. He has attained a Torah of the most inner depths, mingling his breath with the "breath and mouth" of God's word. The story seems to imply that even an ignoramus, or a child of ignoramuses, can attain that status with enough passion and hunger.

The Oral Torah builds on and innovates from the Written Torah and adjusts it to changing times—"rebirths" it, just as R. Yohanan rebirthed R. Eliezer and rebirthed the Jewish people after the destruction of the nation wrought by the Romans.[21] What, though, is the nature of "the truth" that R. Yohanan had taught or, as it were, "given birth to" in R. Eliezer, and what are its costs? The struggle between the heavenly and earthly Torahs plays a central role in the next chapter that focuses on the story of debate over the oven of Akhnai and R. Eliezer's banning.

◦ 2 ◦

"THE GATES OF WOUNDED FEELINGS"

RABBI ELIEZER IS BANNED

> From the day that the Temple was destroyed, prophecy was taken from
> the prophets, but not from the Rabbis.
>
> —*Bava Batra* 12a.

T HE Talmudic tractate *Pirkei Avot*, "The Ethics of the Fathers," ascribes
the following saying to R. Eliezer ben Hyrcanus:

> Let the honor of your fellows be as dear to you as your own and do not
> be easily angered. Warm yourself by the fire of the Sages, but beware
> of their glowing embers lest you be burnt—for their bite is the bite of
> a fox, their sting is the sting of a scorpion, their hiss is the hiss of the
> serpent, and all their words are like fiery coals. (*Pirkei Avot* 2:10)

That sting and that fire permeate the story we will look at in this chapter: R.
Eliezer's traumatic argument with his colleagues at the rabbinic court and
academy at Yavneh which resulted in his being banned. This story, known
as "The Oven of Akhnai," is one of the most famous in all rabbinic literature.[1] I have always been intrigued, like many other contemporary commentators, by its ringing affirmation, *lo ba-shamayim hi*—the Torah "is not
in heaven!" In its original biblical context, this quote from Deuteronomy
30:12 is part of a comforting promise to the Jewish people that they will

return from exile and to God, in love, to enjoy abundant divine blessings. That text from Scripture continues:

> For this commandment which I command you this day, is not hidden from you, nor is it far off. It is not in heaven, that you should say, "Who shall go up for us to heaven, and bring it to us, that we may hear it, and do it?" Nor is it on the other side of the sea, that you should say, "Who shall go over the sea for us, and bring it to us, that we may hear it, and do it?" It is very close to you, in your mouth and heart to observe it.

But when R. Yehoshua, R. Eliezer's colleague and opponent in the debate cites the words "it is not in heaven" to refute R. Eliezer at the climactic moment of our story, the phrase does not mean that the heavenly Torah is close to us, but rather that the Sages do not listen to heavenly voices or allow miracles to decide the Torah's meanings. Human debate and discourse and majority rule here override heavenly intervention. So the story is often read as conforming to postmodern views about plurality of interpretation, the "social construction of meaning," and our inability to attain absolute, objective truth. I confess to also having made that argument.[2]

But shifting the focus to the teacher/student relations in the story has also shifted my understanding of this text. To put it another way, how is the teacher/student relation crucially involved in all the abstract questions of interpretation? For the legal debate in the tale is intertwined with a tragedy in personal relations among teachers, colleagues, and students. The Talmud affirms the connection by inserting the story into a larger discussion of penalties for *ona'at devarim* (wronging another, hurting feelings through verbal injury). This is also a pedagogical story par excellence, widely disseminated and discussed among those even without much acquaintance with Jewish sources. Its drama, imagery, astonishing climax, and denouement make it a highly teachable text. The narrative is rich and has been endlessly analyzed. My discussion here will be oriented towards its relations to the story of R. Eliezer's beginnings from chapter 1—and the story of his passing, which we will look at in chapter 3. In "The Oven of Akhnai" story, R. Eliezer again struggles with the fundamental elements of earth and heaven, and with his status as a student, colleague, and teacher. Once more, R. Eliezer is isolated and in tension with his colleagues; here, too, he gives up everything for *his* Torah; here, too, he is sucked empty.

Here is "The Oven of Akhnai" story from the Talmudic tractate *Bava Metzi'a* 58a-59b:

> R. Hanina, son of R. Idi, said: "What is meant by the verse, 'You shall not wrong one another'—Wrong not a people that are with you in learning and good deeds." Rav said: "One should always be careful of wronging his wife, for since her tears are frequent she is quickly hurt." R. Eleazar said: "Since the destruction of the Temple, the gates of prayer are locked, for it is written, 'Also when I cry out, he shuts out my prayer' [Lam. 3:8]. Yet though the gates of prayer are locked, the gates of tears are not, for it is written, 'Hear my prayer, O Lord, and give ear to my cry; to my tears, be not silent.'" [Ps. 39:13]
>
> . . . R. Hisda said: "All gates are locked, except those through which pass the cries of wronging [ona'ah] . . . ."
>
> . . . We learnt elsewhere: If he cut it into separate segments [huliyot (segmented horizontal rings)], placing sand between each segment, R. Eliezer declared it clean [tahor], and the Sages declared it unclean [tame']. And this was the oven of Akhnai. Why the oven of "Akhnai"? Said Rav Yehudah in Shemuel's name: "Because they encompassed it with arguments like this snake [akhnai], and proved it unclean."
>
> It has been taught: On that day R. Eliezer brought forth every imaginable argument, but the other Sages did not accept them. Said he to them: "If the *halakhah* [legal decision] agrees with me, let this carob-tree prove it!" The carob-tree was uprooted a hundred cubits from its place—others say four hundred cubits.
>
> They retorted: "No proof can be brought from a carob-tree." Again he said: "If the *halakhah* agrees with me, let the stream of water prove it!" The stream of water then flowed backwards.
>
> They said to him: "No proof can be brought from a stream of water."
>
> Again he said: "If the *halakhah* agrees with me, let the walls of the study house prove it!" The walls leaned to fall. But R. Yehoshua rebuked the walls, saying: "If scholars are trouncing each other [menatzhim] in halakhic debate, who are you to interfere?" So they did not fall, in honor of R. Yehoshua, nor did they straighten up, in honor of R. Eliezer. And so they are still standing—leaning.
>
> Again he said to them: "If the *halakhah* agrees with me, let it be proved from Heaven!" A heavenly voice then cried out: "Why do you

dispute with R. Eliezer seeing that the *halakhah* agrees with him in every place!"

R. Yehoshua arose and exclaimed: "It is not in heaven!" [Deut. 30:12].

What did he mean by this? R. Yeremiah said: "That the Torah has already been given at Mount Sinai. We pay no attention to a heavenly voice, because You already wrote in the Torah at Mount Sinai, 'After the majority one should incline'"[Exod. 23:2].

R. Natan met Elijah and asked him: "What did the Holy One, blessed be He, do in that hour?" "He smiled," he replied, "and said, 'My sons have defeated Me, My sons have defeated Me [*nitzhuni banai*].'"

It was said: On that day all objects which R. Eliezer had declared clean were brought and burnt in a fire.

Then they took a vote and blessed him [euphemism for "banned"].

They said, "Who shall go and inform him?" R. Akiva answered, "I will go, lest an unsuitable person go and inform him, and thus destroy the whole world."

What did R. Akiva do? He dressed in black garments, and wrapped himself in black, and sat at a distance of four cubits from him. R. Eliezer asked him, "Akiva, what has particularly happened today?" He replied, "Master, it appears to me that your companions are keeping their distance from you."

Then R. Eliezer, too, rent his clothes, removed his shoes, moved from his seat, and sat on the ground. Tears streamed from his eyes. The world was then smitten: a third of the olive crop, a third of the wheat, and a third of the barley crop. Some say, the dough in women's hands swelled up.

It was taught: Great was the calamity that befell that day, for every place R. Eliezer cast his eyes was burned up. Rabban Gamaliel also was traveling in a ship, and a huge wave arose to drown him. He said, "It appears to me this is on account of none other but R. Eliezer ben Hyrcanus." He then arose and exclaimed, "Master of the Universe! You know full well that I have not acted for my honor, nor for the honor of my father's house, but for Yours, so that strife may not multiply in Israel!" At that, the raging sea subsided.

Imma Shalom was R. Eliezer's wife and the sister of Rabban Gamaliel. From the time of this incident onwards, she did not allow him to fall upon his face [in the special supplication prayer]. Now a certain day happened to be [the holiday of] a New Moon, but she mistook a full month for a defective one [i.e., miscalculated the calendar]. Others say a poor man came and stood at the door, and she took out some bread to him.

When she returned she found him fallen on his face. She said to him: "Arise, you have slain my brother." Meanwhile, an announcement came from the house of Rabban Gamaliel that he had died. He said to her: "From where did you know it?" She said: "I have this tradition from my father's house: 'All gates are locked, except the gates of wounded feelings.'"[3]

Like the story of R. Eliezer's beginnings, this text has an almost surreal quality. One classical rabbinic commentator, R. Shelomo Molkho (1500–1532), even suggests it happened only in a dream of one of the Sages present at the debate. The narrative is intricately wrought; the deeper one delves, the more one becomes entangled in its paradoxes and subtleties— just like the "snake-like" arguments with which the Sages are said to have surrounded the oven and R. Eliezer himself. It is almost like a Rorschach image eliciting the most disparate interpretations and intense passions of its commentators—most fitting for a story which is itself about the stresses of interpretation.

It is often remarked that the story represents a "conservative" R. Eliezer, whose traditions come from a pre-*Hurban* world (i.e., before the destruction of the Second Temple around 70 CE) struggling with colleagues who are trying to refashion a Torah and make interpretive innovations needed to rebuild Jewish life in a new era, after the catastrophes of the Great Revolt against Rome. Seen this way, the debate over the oven is part of a larger ongoing conflict of traditionalists and anti-traditionalist reformers in Yavneh that had already involved a rebellious, temporary overthrow of Rabban Gamaliel (related in *Berakhot* 27b-28a). Rabban Gamaliel was the brother-in-law of R. Eliezer and the second president of the academy and court at Yavneh. He, R. Eliezer, and R. Yehoshua were the three leaders of Yavneh after the death of R. Yohanan ben Zakkai around 90 CE.[4] A close reading of the story, though, complicates matters and raises many questions.

Of all possible issues on heaven and earth over which the Sages might have had such a wrenching and cataclysmic debate, how does a mundane oven become the center of the storm? And what is the relation of the technical legal status of this small oven to the larger religious, pedagogical, and sociological issues at play in this tale? Why, of the scores of disputes recorded in the Mishnah and Talmud between R. Eliezer and his colleagues—from the first page of the Talmud onwards (*Berakhot* 2a)—is *this* the particular issue through which the crisis occurs? Or, to put it another way, why is this particular topic chosen by the editors and storytellers to frame a major trauma in rabbinic history? What prompts these intense passions in a drama that ends tragically with R. Eliezer's banning and separation from his colleagues and students? Isn't the reaction disproportionate to the case in question? Most commentators choose to explicate either the technical legal issue or the philosophical issues. Only a few try to connect them.[5] But I think one cannot grasp the story without attempting to do so, as difficult or speculative as any answer might be. Common to all levels of the story are issues of joining/separation, inside/outside, wholeness/brokenness, heavenly/earthly. But how might they all fit together?

To attempt an answer to these questions, we have to back up a few steps. We need to start by first understanding the legal level of discussion on its own terms. After that comes the midrashic level and the search for what deeper meanings the story might allude to. Jewish thought does not ever allegorize away the legal deliberations; they stand always in their concrete meanings even as other connections are uncovered. The same ancient Sages created both the law and the lore, the halakhic and the aggadic parts of the Talmud and midrash; and those texts, in turn, contain allusions to the esoteric and mystical speculations of Kabbalah. The midrashic portions often contain profound theological speculations framed as parables, analogies, and riddles.[6] All these levels enfold one upon the other like the skin of an onion.

What are these laws of "ritual purity and impurity" in the debate over the status of the oven of Akhnai all about? They were especially important when the Temple in Jerusalem stood, but after its destruction, many of them could no longer be applied. There was no longer a functioning set of Temple sacrifices, or priests, or the cleansing ritual of the "red heifer" (Num. 19:2). On one level, the ongoing interpretation of these laws kept a link to the pre-destruction reality of the holy national and metaphysical center, even if only through legal debate, memory, and hope. But these continued passionate debates were not merely intellectual or legalistic; they also became substitute religious rituals of the "imagined" Temple. And they extended the laws from the destroyed Temple into the domain of daily, ordinary life—the kitchen, hearth, and home, which were purported to have now become a "miniature" Temple.

The Talmud's literary reworking of these laws is a profound religious gesture connecting past and future, ruined and rebuilt Temple, wound and healing. These debates also innovate; they reconfigure religious reality in the current situation, bring life to what had been destroyed. On another level, the laws of ritual purity and impurity (*taharah* and *tumah*) are themselves a way to conceptualize relations between heaven and earth, life and death, closeness to and distance from holiness in the natural world. There can be many causes of *tumah* (ritual impurity), but the chief cause in Jewish law is contact with a dead body, with that which is opposite of life.[7] So I hope the reader will patiently bear with me as I try to clarify the legal issue at stake with our particular oven of Akhnai. The Talmud assumes a reader who already knows this legal background and so does not make it explicit. But even an experienced Talmud student has to wrestle with this complex "serpentine" text.

THE WHOLE AND THE BROKEN; TUMAH AND TAHARAH

What did that oven look like, first of all? These ancient ovens were made of baked clay and fashioned like moveable, large circular pots, narrow at the top and wider on the bottom. The bottom was a large flat surface; and bread was baked in them by sticking it to the sides of the oven; they were also plastered to keep in the heat. Chapters 4 and 5 of the Mishnah's tractate *Kelim*, "Vessels," deal with laws of purity and impurity of vessels and discuss objects that potentially can be susceptible to *tumah* (not all vessels are) and how to purify those that have already acquired *tumah*. Most important for our purposes are the rules that (1) clay vessels are susceptible to *tumah* only when they are *whole* and *complete* (*Kelim* 4:4–5); and (2) if an oven has become impure, it can be purified only by breaking (see also *Kelim* 2:2).

How does one break and reconstruct the oven? The Mishnah prescribes scraping off the plaster holding it together, and then cutting the oven widthwise into small sections. One then removes these sections one by one and reconstructs the oven, placing one segment on top of the other with plaster in between and around the wall of the segments to rejoin them into a whole. After this breaking and reconstructing, the oven is reheated and is usable again for cooking. But note well: once it is considered a complete vessel and purified, it also is now again "susceptible to becoming *tame'*." In other words, the oven is now "pure" and can remain so for a long while, but it is susceptible to *tumah* again if it comes in contact with various *tame'* or impure objects. This is the position of the R. Eliezer's opponents when they proclaim in the story that the oven is impure, *tame'*.

What deeper meanings might lie behind these laws and procedures? The legal texts of the Mishnah are apodictic; they merely state the rules but don't give overt reasons for them. Midrashic, philosophical and kabbalistic speculations often suggest meanings, while maintaining that ultimately one can't fully comprehend them. But *taharah* seems associated with what is still open, incomplete; *tumah* with what is finished, completed, and so without an opening to heaven, to what is beyond human power. Thus a dead body is the principle cause of *tumah*—ultimate completion and closure.

According to Jewish law, one breaks the *tame'* oven to purify it and return it to a state of incompleteness; one can also use living waters to purify certain *tame'* objects, as *taharah* seems to come from ongoing flow. Psychologically, I wonder if this principle might explain the intense vitality we always feel in the middle of the process of creation, when we mentally struggle to give birth to something or work out an insight. Once the goal is attained and completed, the fascination, pleasure, and energy dissipate, and our interest dwindles. Oral Torah itself attempts to keep the closed, finished Written Torah open and connected to the Source from which it flows. Our story seems to rhetorically enact and emblematize this "incompleteness," since it itself has generated endless interpretations. But one feels that something remains incomplete or insufficient in all of them—including my own, I admit! And the vigorous debate about the meaning of our story continues to this day, be it among contemporary secular academic scholars, rabbis, or lay readers.[8]

The laws of *tumah* and *taharah* can certainly be confusing, especially in this story. We need another step to further connect them to the great drama between R. Eliezer and his colleagues. In their typical fashion the Rabbis consider various legal hypotheses, test cases, and practical variations: What, they ask, if one reconstructed an oven that functions and will cook food, but something different was used to glue the segments together in the repair process; is it still to be considered a *complete vessel*? The Mishnah considers the case where *sand* is the medium used to rejoin the segments, which are then afterwards cemented together with plaster. Is that kind of entity now a single unity, a "whole" vessel? Does the sand sufficiently join the segments into a unity, or not? Are the segments still really separated, or practically speaking, is it once again complete and ready for use? The Mishnah identifies *this* case as the "oven of Akhnai."[9] We now have the clue to the identity of our case and a key to decipher the dispute from the story in tractate *Bava Metzi'a* 59a-b:

> We learnt elsewhere: If he cut it into separate segments [*huliyot* (segmented horizontal rings)], placing sand between each segment, R. Eliezer declared it clean [*tahor*], and the Sages declared it unclean [*tame'*]. And this was the oven of Akhnai. Why the oven of "Akhnai"? Said Rav Yehudah in Shemuel's name: "Because they encompassed it with arguments like this snake [*akhnai*], and proved it unclean."
>
> It has been taught: On that day R. Eliezer brought forth every imaginable argument, but they did not accept them.

When the Sages in our story here declare the oven *tame'*, they mean it is indeed to be *considered a whole vessel and thus susceptible* to becoming *tame'*. R. Eliezer is arguing: No, this kind of vessel can NOT be considered whole; and therefore it is NOT susceptible to *tumah* and is in the category of *tahor* (pure). No matter what objects contact or fall into it, even those which might be *tame'*, the foods cooked in it and the oven will never be susceptible to *tumah*.

So what is so important about this issue? Practically speaking, it means that those who followed the Sages' view would not be able to eat or use any of the food or vessels from an Akhnai type of oven under R. Eliezer's supervision. They would fear that these foods could have acquired *tumah* and not been purified, and would therefore be forbidden. *But is this a matter of cosmic importance?* We are still left with our question: Why does R. Eliezer so stubbornly insist on his stance, and why does even Heaven agree with him, but his colleagues nevertheless refuse? And not only refuse, but they also burn *all the objects* he has declared pure and ostracize him? What snake in the garden causes this expulsion and its terrible consequences?

Some readers argue that these seemingly arcane technical questions dealing with the ritual purity and impurity of the oven are just a pretext for the larger debate about interpretive authority of the Torah brewing in a new post-destruction era. In other words, it would not matter *what* issue was being debated; the explosion was ready to occur and was inevitable. Or we could follow a contemporary academic approach and argue that there is no accurate portrayal of any specific historical events here, but only a literary dramatization of an ideological conflict.[10] Nevertheless, we are still left with the question: Why choose this particular legal issue to frame that great conflict? I sense that these exacting, seemingly dry legal definitions are deftly chosen and woven into the Talmud's narrative of the debate as parts of a psychological, historical, and religious drama. For among the underlying questions of the Talmudic story's drama and cast of characters are: Who really is "pure"? And how do we know? Which intentions are "pure"? And how can formally pure acts, deeds, intentions become susceptible to "impurity" in their effects? And once impure, how can they be mended? What really constitutes unity? When a person or relationship or nation is broken, or relations between heaven and earth are torn, how can there be reconstruction? And what are the costs?

In other words, the question of division and unity in the oven's segments would also offer a subtle but concrete embodiment of "separation and wholeness" on so many other levels of the story: in personal and family relations, teacher/student and collegial relations, the political and metaphysical relations between heaven and earth, and between Torah and its interpreters—all of which fracture. Unity is broken up—like the segments of the oven. In short, I suggest that the story's technical arguments about "purity and impurity" and their consequences reflect broader dilemmas.

The narrative indeed probes the limits of dissent in rabbinic culture as it struggles to rebuild after catastrophe and put itself, the people, and the nation back together (like the oven). Can the nation, can the people, can the Rabbis' attempts at spreading holiness and actualizing God's presence and will in the world . . . can they ever be the same again? And if not, what needs to be done? What kind of Torah is needed now? At the same time, the story is also a brave self-critique of rabbinic culture. Who indeed is the hero? Who does the right thing, but perhaps in the wrong way?[11]

R. Yosef Eliyahu Henkin, a modern Jewish Orthodox halakhic expert, also asks how so seemingly minor an issue could have led to such an exaggerated response—the banning and pain of R. Eliezer, the shaking of heaven and earth, and the death of Rabban Gamaliel who was the head of the rabbinic academy. This "astonishing story," he writes,

> is enveloped in darkness . . . it must be that this was a matter upon which the continued existence of Israel depended, and not just any ordinary argument. But the Sages enclothed and concealed it in layers of *aggadah* [non-legal dramatic tales], as is their way, for the sake of peace.[12]

There was indeed a fierce and highly personal and ideological debate, one which dealt with fatal issues and had terrible consequences. But the Sages did not want to state it overtly "for the sake of peace"—by which R. Henkin means, I suspect, not to malign the participants of the debate and cause its continuation, or reveal publicly what should not be revealed. In other words, it was an issue too highly charged to be presented directly due to the damage it could cause. We might push R. Henkin's insight a bit further, or translate it into more contemporary vocabulary and speculate that Talmudic narrative, like a Freudian dream process, has condensed and displaced the events, censored parts of them, and reworked everything through images and drama to convey a difficult message. What could it have been?

Aggadic narratives, by definition, such as "The Oven of Akhnai," need to be read on more than the "literal" level—whether it be the "literal" of a fundamentalist non-critical reading (it all "really" happened just as they are describing), or the "literal" of a historicist reading (the meaning is to be found by a critical-empirical attempt to reconstruct the texts' composition and redaction). The Talmudic narrators and editors did not intend or attempt to write history in our modern, impersonal, objective sense. They probed the religious meanings of events the Jewish people had endured. They constructed and inscribed meanings not only for their own generation, but also for future ones. *Toledot* is the Hebrew word for "history," and also means "engenderment, generation." What, they also ask, do all the turbulent and traumatic events suffered bring forth, engender, in the ongoing mission of Israel? How might the texts, stories, and commentaries already handed down also contain clues to that future?

R. Henkin, though neither an academic historian nor a political ideologue, refers us to the story's historical context: the fierce first and second century debates among Jews whether or not to rebel once more against the Roman occupation. The story indeed is set during a time of Roman oppression and loss of political sovereignty after the destruction of the Temple. The consequences of that trauma have been strongly felt through the subsequent two-thousand-year period of the Jews' exile from their land that began then. Even later editors of the Talmud still grapple with the catastrophes of that period, as do contemporary observant Jews who, to this day, fast and mourn annually on the Hebrew date the Temple was destroyed (9 Av) as required by Jewish law.

We'll remember from chapter 1, the famous story of R. Eliezer helping smuggle his teacher, the religious leader R. Yohanan ben Zakkai, out of besieged Jerusalem, around the year 70 CE. In that story, R. Yohanan understands the futility of the revolt against Rome and its brutal legions, but the Jewish political and military rebels who have been fighting and have taken control of Jerusalem violently oppose anyone who tries to negotiate peace. R. Yohanan, upon his escape, hails the Roman general and future emperor Vespasian, and asks to be allowed to rebuild his rabbinic academy and court on the coast in Yavneh. R. Eliezer becomes one of its pillars, along with his great student R. Akiva in the succeeding generation. R. Henkin argues that the "concealed" debate that arouses such passions in our story was the question of whether to attempt another revolt against Rome and restore Jewish political sovereignty. Historically, there were in fact two other revolts against Rome in the sixty tumultuous and disastrous years after the first one failed in 72 CE. These fierce rebellions against the Roman generals and later emperors Trajan and Hadrian had temporary successes, including a few years of restored Jewish political sovereignty and the recapture of Jerusalem. But ultimately they failed and caused further massive destruction, slaughter, expulsion, and slavery, especially the last revolt of Shimon bar Kokhba between 132 and 135 CE. So this ongoing debate indeed was an issue upon which the continued existence of Israel depended. It was a life and death matter for the Jewish people.

In R. Henkin's interpretation, R. Eliezer, as the great disciple of R. Yohanan ben Zakkai, was opposed to another revolt; he thought it would not succeed in the end, and even if there were temporary triumphs, no lasting and enduring sovereignty could be sustained. He feared more disasters and the further decimation of the Jewish people. The oven's cut-up segments rejoined with sand allude, in this reading, to an attempt to set up political sovereignty from the now dismembered nation. But in R. Eliezer's view, the sand prevents these segments from fully joining to become a complete vessel, i.e., constituting a true, enduring, political sovereignty.

R. Henkin's interpretation has many other supporting arguments that may or may not convince its readers. I don't have the space to discuss those details here, but it is striking that when we think today about what most inflames the passion of Jews, creates bitter personal and intense disputes amongst them, and between Israel and the nations of the world, it is a similar debate over political sovereignty of Jews in the land of Israel. What are the rights of the Jews to their own independent nation and to what lengths should they go to defend it? To what extent should they take up weapons and conduct wars over it? To what extent should they be obedient to dictates of the great imperial powers or the United Nations? Where should they compromise, and where should they remain inflexible? What will ensure the nation's existence, and what will endanger it? It's not coincidental that R. Henkin wrote his article shortly after the Six-Day War in June 1967 when the question of Israeli sovereignty over a mass of newly conquered territories had already arisen. In such arguments, colleagues can indeed become enemies, verbal wronging flourishes, one side ostracizes the other, and bitterness infects personal relations among families, teachers, and students, and causes irreparable damage. The consequences of this debate are fateful for the life and death of the people and the nation.[13]

Whether or not one agrees with R. Henkin's interpretation, the Talmudic narrative makes clear a darker side to the dispute when it interprets the name of the purported owner of the oven, "Akhnai," as a reference to the word for "snake."[14] Not only is the oven of Akhnai surrounded by sinewy, snake-like arguments, but so is R. Eliezer himself. The classical Talmudic commentator known by the acronym "Rashi" (R. Shelomo ben Yitzhak, 1040–1105) astutely notes that a snake tends to wrap itself around things and take on a circular form, putting its tail in its mouth. A snake, of course, also kills with its mouth. In the Oral Torah, the Torah of the Mouth, there is a potentially dangerous snake. The place where the human mouth creates Torah, where human reason can illumine, where "interpretive communities" can build worlds, can also be the place of deadly verbal wronging.[15]

On one level, we could see the story as again engaging the question of the right balance between the "plastered cistern" and "welling spring." R. Eliezer is steadfast and faithful to his traditions here, though he also calls upon supernatural proofs which reverse natural processes. Is the problem that faithfulness to past tradition becomes unfaithfulness to pressing realities—making the waters "flow backwards" instead of forwards, uprooting rather than planting? Does the vessel now need to be broken open to give forth, to create something new? Revolutionaries and romantics opt for breaking. But there is great peril in ignoring the question: What are the costs of the breaking? And once broken, how can things and relationships be put back together? And if so, are they ever the same? These ethical and interpretive questions may be abstract, but I think this narrative enacts various alternative scenarios through the literary drama that runs as counterpoint to the logical surface arguments. Like life, these scenarios and their various outcomes are filled with paradox. Jeffrey Rubenstein sums up some of the tensions in his literary analysis of the story:

> Although the miracles and heavenly voice prove that Eliezer's halakhic ruling is "objectively" true in that it conforms with the divine will, it is not legally valid. God entrusted the Torah to the Sages to administer and interpret, and they must render decisions according to the legal process, namely the decision of the majority. The Sages, paradoxically, have the authority to ignore the divine will. Their interpretation, not the original, authorial intention, established the meaning.[16]

THE TEARS OF R. ELIEZER

It appears that when all the rational and logical arguments have been exhausted, R. Eliezer suddenly moves beyond the realm of tradition and logic and resorts to supernatural "proofs": uprooted trees, backwards-flowing water, shaking walls of the study house. These visual images of shaking and uprooting are emblems of the tremors and rifts occurring ideologically and personally in the academy. Earth, air, trees, walls, water—these are all also the fundamental elements of creation. He has struggled "for his ground" from the story of his beginnings onward, and here once again, he tries to "hold his ground." It's a climactic moment, similar to the story of his beginnings. When pressed by R. Yohanan and his colleagues to "open," he publicly teaches and interprets for the first time. Then, too, he suddenly reaches supernal realms and utters things never heard before. But here even his miraculous proofs involve things that literally lose their ground. And just as he was uprooted from his biological family in his youth, he will now again be uprooted, like the carob-tree, from his place in the circle of scholars and academy.[17]

R. Eliezer physically falls back to the ground twice: the first time from the ban under which he is put; the second time when he performs the prayer of "falling on the face," which inadvertently leads to the death of his wife's brother, Rabban Gamaliel. As the successor to R. Yohanan ben Zakkai and head (nasi) of the Sanhedrin, the High Court at Yavneh, Rabban Gamaliel had to approve the ban of R. Eliezer. There is a difference between a rabbinic "ban" (niddui) and the much more severe decree of "excommunication" (herem). Niddui was imposed only for a specified number of days after which it could be then be renewed. But during that time no one, except for family members, was allowed to socially associate with or be closer than four cubits (approximately 6 feet) from the banned person. All the laws of a mourner applied to the one who was banned: he or she must sit on the ground, not wear shoes, not have a haircut, and so forth. If the person died during the ban, a stone had to be put on the bier, and relatives were not obligated to tear their garments as in the usual practice of mourning.

Was R. Eliezer banned or was he excommunicated? There is much debate and commentary. Rashi, for example, writes that R. Eliezer was banned; Maimonides, however, thinks it was the more severe form of excommunication.[18] In either case, once again R. Eliezer "loses his place." And "place" is one of the repetitive key words in the narrative, as are the movements of "sitting," "standing," and "falling." How are his colleagues and students going to handle this fall? R. Akiva, R. Eliezer's great student, volunteers to inform him of the ban; he recognizes the great danger both to the world and to R. Eliezer's honor. Then begins their dramatic encounter. R. Akiva dresses in black and sits at the prescribed distance from R. Eliezer. It is almost as if R. Akiva takes on R. Eliezer's identity, mirrors him in a mute gesture of closeness and distance at once. R. Shemuel Eidels (1555–1631), also known as "Maharsha" and one of the classic Talmudic commentators, perceptively notes that R. Akiva dresses and acts as if *he* is in niddui and has been banned, not R. Eliezer.

> It was said: On that day all objects which R. Eliezer had declared clean were brought and burnt in a fire.
> Then they took a vote and blessed him [euphemism for "banned"].

They said, "Who shall go and inform him?" R. Akiva answered, "I will go, lest an unsuitable person go and inform him, and thus destroy the whole world."

What did R. Akiva do? He dressed in black garments, and wrapped himself in black, and sat at a distance of four cubits from him. R. Eliezer asked him, "Akiva, what has particularly happened today?" He replied, "Master, it appears to me that your companions are keeping their distance from you."

Then R. Eliezer, too, rent his clothes, removed his shoes, moved from his seat, and sat on the ground. Tears streamed from his eyes. The world was then smitten: a third of the olive crop, a third of the wheat, and a third of the barley crop. Some say, the dough in women's hands swelled up.

Perhaps R. Akiva is already mourning for his personal loss or the loss of R. Eliezer's Torah; or perhaps he is enacting a kind of symbolic death along with his teacher. Only a student so close could approach him with the news. Only one so close could understand the great pain and danger, and partake of it with his teacher. R. Eliezer has been transformed suddenly into a teacher who cannot teach, isolated from his colleagues. Once again he is in a liminal space, that of the mourner. Once again, he loses speech, is muted. And once again, stores of food and the nourishment essential to life are endangered. His words do not destroy the crops—the food—but his glance does; his tears and pain are acknowledged only by God and the elements.

He is a kind of King Lear on the heath. His tears become a force that swells the seas, break through natural boundaries. Here the scale tips dangerously back once again: his colleagues "outweighed" him in the debate, but his cry of pain inadvertently threatens to destroy the world's sources of nurture and life. The balance needs to be restored; a woman enters:

Imma Shalom was R. Eliezer's wife, and the sister of Rabban Gamaliel. From the time of this incident onwards, she did not allow him to fall upon his face [in the special supplication prayer]. Now a certain day happened to be New Moon, but she mistook a full month for a defective one. Others say, a poor man came and stood at the door, and she took out some bread to him.

When she returned she found him fallen on his face. She said to him: "Arise, you have slain my brother." Meanwhile, an announcement came from the house of Rabban Gamaliel that he had died. He said to her: "From where did you know it?" She said: "I have this tradition from my father's house: 'All gates are locked, except the gates of wounded feelings.'"

Into this world of *mahaloket*—a world of male dispute—suddenly appears R. Eliezer's wife, Imma Shalom, who is also the sister of Rabban Gamaliel. "Imma Shalom" literally means "Mother of Peace." Her intervention is not the serpentine, raging textual debate of the men, nor one of thunderous miracles, but a tradition she has from her father's house about the "gates of wounded feelings." It's a kind of "Torah of the Mothers," an Oral Torah passed down from parent to child, face-to-face, equally powerful and living. This same tradition was cited by R. Eleazar and R. Hisda right before the story plunges suddenly into the dispute over the oven.

The debate, we remember, is inserted into a larger overall Talmdic discussion of penalties for *ona'at devarim* (wronging another, hurting feelings through verbal injury).

> R. Eleazar said: "Since the destruction of the Temple, the gates of prayer are locked, for it is written, 'Also when I cry out, he shuts out my prayer.' Yet though the gates of prayer are locked, the gates of tears are not, for it is written, 'Hear my prayer, O Lord, and give ear unto my cry.'" . . . R. Hisda said: "All gates are locked, except the gates [through which pass] the cries of wrong [*ona'ah*]."

With Imma Shalom's appearance and her citation of this tradition again, the story circles back on itself to remind us of this larger context. It jolts us into further questioning which side should have our sympathies. There are unforeseen consequences to these ideological conflicts and legal distinctions, and pure intentions may have devastating human results. Who is right here?

"IT IS NOT IN HEAVEN"

The loss of the Temple has closed many gates to heaven, including gates of prayer. The men have been arguing, trying to find other openings and to rebuild a Torah to ensure that the Jewish people survive in a different world. Underlying the debate is a deep division over the kind of Torah it will be. R. Yehoshua, Rabbi Eliezer's colleague, rises. Both had stood on opposite sides of the false bier of R. Yohanan ben Zakkai to smuggle him out of Jerusalem. Now both stand on opposite sides of the debate:

> R. Yehoshua arose and exclaimed: "It is not in heaven!" [Deut. 30:12].
> What did he mean by this? R. Yeremiah said: "That the Torah has already been given at Mount Sinai. We pay no attention to a heavenly voice, because You already wrote in the Torah at Mount Sinai, 'After the majority one should incline'" [Exod. 23:2].
> R. Natan met Elijah and asked him: "What did the Holy One, blessed be He, do in that hour?" "He smiled," he replied, "and said, 'My sons have defeated Me, My sons have defeated Me.'"

But we might wonder what kind of smile it was. One of pleasure and affirmation—or of irony—or both?

Through Imma Shalom we are reminded that there is a different, direct line to heaven—the gates of prayer are fully open when the cries of those who have been wronged rise up. R. Eliezer's wife is indeed the one trying to keep peace, *shalom*, through her sensitivity to his feelings—but she cannot control the outcome. She knows the dangers of his mute pain and frustration and prevents him from performing the special supplicatory prayer of "falling on the face." (As later codified, this was the place in the daily liturgy for personal petitionary prayer and begins with leaning one's head on the left arm and covering the face.)

R. Eliezer's "falling on the face" here is also metaphorically synonymous with his shame and pain. It is also the intimate, personal place where he is heard by God, where R. Eliezer's power, truth, and purity are still acknowledged. God hears the pain of the one wronged by words (*ona'at devarim*). But R. Eliezer may also be crying for what he sees as the truth, for the loss of the pure truth of a heavenly Torah. Rabban Gamaliel had the authority as head of the Sanhedrin to put R. Eliezer under the ban and claims he had to do so for the sake of unity in Israel. His death, however, does not ensure unity for all. When he dies, a family fractures. R. Eliezer's words of prayer have unintentionally had a lethal effect—ironically another "wounding through words."

Imma Shalom does not need official announcements or proclamations to know this: "Arise, you have slain my brother." And with this falling, he also "rises," with all the paradoxes and double meanings this moment entails. Just as the literary images can bear opposite meanings, so the story deals simultaneously with equal and conflicting truths. However, the narrative does not negate the need for a practical legal decision by the majority, despite the consequences and pain caused. But neither can that pain and that other truth go unacknowledged, nor can limits and boundaries be violated without consequences.

What has happened to the relations between teachers and students in the story? Daniel Greenwood, a legal theorist, writes in his analysis that it is no accident that all the major players are intimately related. For this is also a "family dispute, not an abstract debate over universal principles."[19] In the story, knowledge and Torah are not abstract epistemology, or only political ideology—but constructed in living personal relations between students and teachers, in a community of colleagues.

As Greenwood puts it in summarizing the story's paradoxes, multiple perspectives, and serpentine layers of meanings:

> Akhnai teaches, I think, that truth and peace are often incompatible, and that we must respect both; that one must follow the majority even when it is wrong, but that one may not follow the majority to do evil; that mutual respect is more important than reaching the right answer; and that we should treat the law as an inheritance, but it is nonetheless our inheritance, and we must be the ones deciding to treat it as such. It shows us determinacy coming out of an indeterminate law; interpretation creating radical new meanings where there were none, or few, before; the struggle to find the mechanisms of change that alone can keep the Law constant; and, not least important, the struggles of competing commitments, to God, community, husband, and brother. The Mother of Peace fails to make peace here, but she understands the principle: not principles but relationships will do it.[20]

All true, but the personal relations do not hinder the necessary legal decision, nor do they overthrow it in the story. The Sages' legal decision does stand; neither they nor R. Eliezer recant. But on other levels of the story, the sympathies of the narrator—and God—move with R. Eliezer. Who indeed is the "hero" of this story?

The oppositions, the extreme swings of life and death, heaven and earth, the natural and the supernatural, the male and female principles, need to come to some kind of balance; they may not be resolvable, but if not balanced they become destructive. Only the walls of the "study house," the story tells us, remain "still standing—leaning" between the opposing positions, precariously balanced. Perhaps because only the study house can contain these oppositions:

> Again he said: "If the *halakhah* agrees with me, let the walls of the study house prove it!" The walls leaned to fall. But R. Yehoshua rebuked the walls, saying: "If scholars are trouncing each other [*menatzhim*] in halakhic debate, who are you to interfere?" So they did not fall, in honor of R. Yehoshua, nor did they straighten up, in honor of R. Eliezer. And so they are still standing—leaning.

In refuting R. Eliezer, the Sages cite the biblical commandment to "incline [*sic*] after the majority" (Exod. 23:2). But in those "inclining" walls, standing so until today, in the continuous rereading and reinterpreting of the story, in teachers' and students' ritualized study of it, all the opposing opinions can co-exist. "Both these and these are the words of the living God, but the *halakhah* is according to Hillel" as the famous Talmudic statement puts it (*Eruvin* 13b). In other words, without the two sides, there is not a "living" God, but a dead one.

R. Yehudah Amital, a modern Israeli commentator, understands the debate about the oven on a deeper level, as reflecting two different worldviews, two notions of truth. Our world is one of duality, strife, and division. The oven of Akhnai, similarly, was constructed from many pieces:

> *"They cut it into segments and placed sand between them; R. Eliezer declared it pure, while the Sages declared it impure."* In R. Eliezer's view, an oven that is not all a single unit is not to be considered a vessel at all and therefore cannot contract impurity. Even though sand was placed between the segments in order to join them, this was insufficient to change its status into a single vessel, a whole entity. R. Eliezer lived in a utopian world, in which wholeness is absolute. Not so the Sages, who maintain that if the oven is joined together in any manner—even by means of segments connected by layers of sand—then the oven may be considered a "vessel," that is, capable of receiving impurity. They admitted that we live in a world of complexity and imperfection.[21]

R. Amital's reading is a thoughtful attempt to connect the legal and philosophical levels of the story. But of course, there is always another differing rabbinic interpretation; and a radical psychological-theological view of "It is not in heaven" is put forth by the unconventional nineteenth-century Hasidic thinker, R. Tzadok ha-Kohen. R. Eliezer's support from heaven, comments R. Tzadok, does not necessarily mean that he had a higher or more utopian truth (as R. Amital argues), or a more correct one, even if his truth is not practically applicable in this situation. He writes:

> Sometimes someone sees with clarity that God assists and agrees
> with one's actions. But this is not a proof that one's actions are really
> correct. For it is said, "God leads you the way you shall go" (Isa. 48:17).
> And the Sages interpreted this to mean (*Makkot* 10b): "The path that
> a person desires to pursue is the path in which God will direct him."
> And this is what "It is not in heaven" refers to: even though God helped
> R. Eliezer with miracles to show the law was according to him, the
> Sages did not rely on that, for they thought it was because that was the
> path R. Eliezer wished to take.[22]

In other words, in a person's choice of whichever path he or she might take, she or he will obtain assistance from heaven, but that assistance does *not necessarily mean* the action is at bottom the correct one, or even a more pure truth. So although R. Eliezer was assisted from heaven with miracles and a "heavenly voice" (*bat kol*)—that was only due to the particular path he had wanted to take, not necessarily the correct truth. His comment is characteristic of the way kabbalistic and Hasidic thought map many "levels" and "worlds" of truth. In our story, for instance, the terms *bat kol*, "heavenly voice," and "heaven" in the phrase "the Torah is not in heaven," would be read as referring to various "categories" or "spiritual domains" (*behinot*) above which there are many further higher spiritual "worlds." The laws of each spiritual world are unique and do not apply in the others. Each world is "true" to its own laws, i.e., it has its own integral "truth."[23]

In the great ongoing "study house" of the Talmud itself, R. Eliezer will eventually be inserted back into his place. He is cited endless times in the Talmud and Mishnah as a source of opinion, often dissenting.[24] If we would argue, as does R. Amital, that the Sages' majority view in the Akhnai story is pragmatic, necessarily allowing for a world of complexity, duality, and imperfection—then decisions will not always perfectly conform with theory or even truth. The Torah cannot be just in "heaven," and R. Eliezer has to yield his place. But then perhaps that, paradoxically, is also the "heavenly Torah"—the Torah of the God who "smiles" when his sons defeat Him in this argument and a God who yields His own place. That would be another way to understand God's words, "*Nitzhuni banai*" (My sons have defeated me). The consonantal Hebrew root for the verb "to conquer, defeat"—n-tz-h—is also the root of the verb "*nitzeah*" (to make illustrious, to glorify, to eternalize). According to an oft-cited popular rabbinic interpretation, through this double entendre God would be affirming the Sages' assertion that the Torah is "not in heaven." Their endless, ongoing debate in the temporal, finite world is indeed what "eternalizes" it: *Nitzhuni banai*: "My sons have eternalized me."[25]

But if we translate *nitzhuni banai* as "My children have won over me," we would have an additional layer of meaning and another reason for God's smile: they "won me over," i.e., they have won my approval and love. As to why the phrase is repeated *twice* in the story, I do not know—perhaps to hint that, in the end, both opinions are correct: they have "defeated" me and they have "won me over."

Daniel Greenwood suggests in the concluding paragraph of his essay that perhaps God laughed because "the Father saw that His education had worked." His children bested him in argument. And in this time of destruction and the loss of the direct voice of God, the Temple, and the prophets, God's children now

> enter adulthood . . . where we have not answers and paternal guidance, but endless debate . . . hurt feelings, principles we accept as necessary for life together but can not apply . . . political struggles that are not theorized but lived. If stasis and stable law are death, this is life.[26]

But what happens to R. Eliezer, a teacher who has been "made impure"? The story itself does not end with his triumph, but with the death of his brother-in-law and a reminder of the cataclysmic damage done by wounding words and hurt feelings. In the next chapter, we'll witness the replay of his confrontation with the Sages on his death bed and the lifting of the ban in the moment after he dies with the word "*tahor*" (pure) on his lips.

- 3 -

"FATHER! FATHER! ISRAEL'S CHARIOT AND ITS HORSEMEN!"

THE PASSING OF RABBI ELIEZER

> As they kept walking and talking, a fiery chariot with fiery horses sud-
> denly appeared and separated one from the other, and Elijah went up
> to heaven in a whirlwind. Elisha saw it and cried out, "Father! Father!
> Israel's chariot and its horsemen!" When he could no longer see him,
> he grasped his garments and rent them in two.
>
> —2 Kings 2:11–12

Rabbi Eliezer ben Hyrcanus and Elijah were historically separated by almost a thousand years. One was a Sage; the other a prophet. But they share a similar spiritual profile: full of fiery intensity, they were both far more attuned to the purities of heaven than the compromises necessary on earth. And so, the Sage and the prophet became isolated. Each fought for his Torah and each was painfully removed from his role as a teacher of Israel. What happens to great teachers when denied their teaching roles and students? Why do teachers fail, and how do students cope when their teachers pass from the world? The third story I want to examine about R. Eliezer is the narrative of his passing that engages these questions. It is also one of the most poignant in the Talmud.[1] On the verge of death, R. Eliezer's colleagues come to visit him; the old arguments are replayed but with a new twist. He expresses his pain, jousts with them, and breathes his last with the word "*tahor*" (pure) on his lips. The ban finally is lifted . . . but only after he is gone. In this story, "The Oven of Akhnai" is a tense subtext throughout, and R. Eliezer's foremost disciple, R. Akiva, moves to center stage.

Variants of the narrative appear in the Jerusalem Talmud (*Shabbat* 2:6), the midrashic collection *Avot de-Rabbi Natan [A]* 25, and the Babylonian Talmud, *Sanhedrin* 68a. Each version inserts the story into a different context: the first is framed by a discussion of the laws of the Sabbath; the second, a discussion about death; the third, a debate about the laws and penalties for sorcery. Each context tinges the story with a different meaning. The Babylonian Talmud's account is the most developed dramatically and psychologically and is the one I will use here. I make this choice due to the literary and aesthetic qualities of this version and because I am especially intrigued by the relations between sorcery, death, and teaching at which the text hints.

SETTING THE SCENE

The story in *Sanhedrin* 68a is prefaced by a discussion of a tradition from an earlier codification of the Oral Law:

> A sorcerer, if he actually performs magic, is liable [to death], but not if he merely creates illusions. R. Akiva said in R. Yehoshua's name: "Of two who gather cucumbers [by magic] one may be punished and the other exempt. He who really gathers them is punished; while he who only produces an illusion [of doing something when he really does nothing] is exempt."

The Talmud then relates colorful stories of sorcerers, discusses various forms of magic and, in its characteristic style, asks *who* in fact originally taught this law to R. Akiva: Didn't R. Akiva learn this Torah from R. Eliezer and not from R. Yehoshua? R. Yehoshua, we'll remember, was R. Eliezer's fellow student, colleague, and great opponent in the Akhnai debate. What is at stake here? What difference does it make which of the two taught this law to R. Akiva—or if each taught it to him but did so differently with a different "teaching style"?

Instead of a direct answer, the next sentence of the story suddenly transports us to R. Eliezer's sickbed:

But did R. Akiva learn this from R. Yehoshua? For it was taught: When R. Eliezer fell ill, R. Akiva and his colleagues went to visit him. He was seated in his canopied bed [kinof], while they sat in his salon [teraklin]. That day was the eve of the Sabbath, and his son Hyrcanus went in to him to remove his tefillin [phylacteries]. But his father rebuked him harshly, and he retreated crestfallen.

"It appears to me," he said to them, "that my father's mind is deranged [nitrefah]."

But he [R. Eliezer] said to them, "His [Hyrcanus'] mind and his mother's are deranged. How can one neglect a prohibition punishable by stoning, and turn his attention to something only forbidden as a 'shevut'?"

The Sages, seeing that his mind was clear, entered his chamber and sat at a distance of four cubits from him.

"Why have you come?" he said to them.

"We have come to study Torah," they answered.

"And why didn't you come before now?" he asked.

"We had no time," they responded.

He said, "I will be surprised if these die a natural death."

R. Akiva asked, "And what will mine be?"

"Yours will be crueler than theirs," he answered.

He then took his two arms and placed them over his heart, and said: "Woe to you, two arms of mine that are like two Scrolls of the Torah being rolled up. Much Torah I learned and much Torah I taught. Much Torah I learned, but I did not even skim from my teachers as much as a dog licks from the sea. Much Torah I taught, but my disciples only drew from me as much as a painting stick from its tube.

"Not only that, I have studied three hundred laws on the subject of a deep bright spot [a form of leprosy, Lev. 13:2], and no one has ever asked me anything about them. And I have studied three hundred—or, as others state, three thousand laws—about the planting of cucumbers [by magic], and no one ever asked me about them except Akiva ben Yosef.

"Once he and I were walking together on a road, when he said to me, 'My Teacher, teach me about the planting of cucumbers.' I said something, and the whole field was filled with cucumbers. Then he said: 'Teacher, you taught me how to plant them. Now teach me how to uproot them.' I said something and all the cucumbers were gathered in one place."

His visitors then asked him, "A ball, a shoe-form [of a shoemaker], an amulet, a pearl-pouch, and a small weight—what is the law?"

He replied, "They are *tame'* [susceptible to becoming impure], [and if impure] they are restored to their purity [*taharah*] just as they are."

They asked him, "What of a shoe that is on the shoe-form?"

He replied, "*Tahor*" . . . and his soul departed "*be-taharah* [in purity]."

Then R. Yehoshua stood on his feet, and exclaimed, "The vow is annulled, the vow is annulled!"

At the end of the Sabbath, R. Akiva met his bier being carried from Caesarea to Lydda. [In his grief] he beat his flesh until the blood flowed down upon the earth. R. Akiva began his funeral address as the mourners were lined up about the bier, and said: "'My father, my father, the chariot of Israel and its horsemen!' [2 Kings 2:12]. I have many coins, but no money changer to accept them."

So from this story we see that he learned this law from R. Eliezer.—He learned it from R. Eliezer, but did not grasp it, and then he learned it from R. Yehoshua, who made it clear to him.

But how could R. Eliezer perform such an act of sorcery? Didn't we learn, "if he actually performed magic, he is liable"? The answer is that if it is done only to teach, it is permitted, for it has been said, "You shall not learn to do after the abominations of these nations [Deut. 18:9]." This means: you are not permitted to learn in order to perform it, but you are permitted to learn in order to understand and teach. (*Sanhedrin* 68a)

The story does finally answer its initial question—from whom did R. Akiva learn the laws of sorcery, R. Yehoshua or R. Eliezer?—but what a journey it has taken us on! The tale is itself a great "scene of teaching" especially in its combination of narration and dramatic dialogue, use of images, gestures and allusions. But as with every great teaching, much is expressed indirectly, subtly, ironically and requires close scrutiny.

My reading here, as in the previous two chapters, uses formalistic literary methods, combined with speculations about larger existential and theological meanings. My assumption is that the story's editors did not compose its sections or details arbitrarily. And once the story has been handed down, it also takes on its own afterlife. Like the story of R. Eliezer's beginnings and "The Oven of Akhnai," it has all the compression, intensity, and volatility of a dream. As in a dream, the attentive interpreter can sense the way all the details connect under the surface and allude to deeper meanings. But to find those connections and meanings, the interpreter has to first closely scrutinize the details, try several ways of fitting the puzzle together, and patiently wait for a sense of the whole to emerge. And then reread again. So I'll proceed by breaking this complex narrative into scenes, closely analyzing each one, and slowing down our reading to savor the story's rhetorical effects and probe its meanings. This tale is especially suited to such "scripting" due to its highly dramatic character.

Like all Talmudic texts, the story also forces us to ask sharp questions and make judgments. Only through our questions and associations do we reach its profounder levels. As Emmanuel Levinas notes in his astute commentary on the story, its full sense is acquired only through the way the Talmud amplifies the original problem it poses: Did R. Akiva learn the law from R. Yehoshua or R. Eliezer? The meaning comes "by the new questions its own questions will raise, and by the non-spoken meanings that will appear in the meaning it expresses."[2] That process is a fundamental mode of Jewish learning. So let us begin our questioning.

TENSIONS BETWEEN FATHERS AND SONS,
SABBATH AND THE WEEKDAY

> But did R. Akiva learn this from R. Yehoshua? For it was taught that when R. Eliezer fell sick, R. Akiva and his companions went in to visit him. He sat in his canopied four-poster bed [kinof], while they sat in his outer salon [teraklin].

This physical separation between the visiting Sages and R. Eliezer also represents their intellectual, spiritual, and physical separation since his being banned. His bed is described as kinof, "canopied," a small detail which increases the sense of his isolation. Canopied beds have curtains to screen them. His bed is situated in a room at the end of the salon, whose door opens on to it. In the Hebrew word used for "salon" here—teraklin (apparently from the Latin triclinium)—the proficient Talmud student might hear an echo of the famous passage in Pirkei Avot 4:16: "Rabbi Ya'akov said, 'This world is like a corridor [prozdor] before the World to Come. Prepare yourself in the foyer, so that you will be able to enter the salon [teraklin].'" This language and the geographical setting place R. Eliezer on the verge of death, soon to enter his next world. Once more, he is in a liminal, transitional space.

The canopied bed is a kind of reverse image of the special exalted place he had held in the rabbinic academy before the ban. Even though R. Eliezer's status has now been inverted, he still strongly propounds his legal verdicts from this "high place." He does not "go gentle into that good night," to use the poet Dylan Thomas' famous words, but will "rage, rage against the dying of the light." Repeated verbs of sitting and standing echo throughout the story and parallel the "sitting, standing, falling" verbal patterns in the story of his banning in "The Oven of Akhnai," *Bava Metzi'a* 58a-59b.

Scene 1: "That day was the eve of the Sabbath"

The narrator now indicates the time frame: another transitional moment. Moving from the last day of the week into the Sabbath is a major transition in every Jewish household. The Sabbath is a different realm of time and space—of rest, holiness, and pleasure—and is compared to a "taste of the World to Come." Yonah Fraenkel, in his commentary on the shorter version of this story in the Jerusalem Talmud, also perceives how this specific timing-setting of the Sabbath eve embodies the momentous approach of R. Eliezer's death. In that version of the story, the narrator immediately reveals to us that "he was critically ill." It begins with the words: "A story of R. Eliezer who was expiring [*goses*] on the eve of the Sabbath at nightfall . . . " (Jerusalem Talmud, *Shabbat* 2:6).[3]

The teller of the Babylonian Talmud's version builds the tension gradually, and we infer the gravity of the situation more slowly. Both versions make us feel the tension in time. As Fraenkel writes, the set halakhic time of the closely approaching Sabbath is in tension with the lapsing, uncertain time of R Eliezer's life: Nightfall is indeed coming on two levels. The eve of the Sabbath is also always a pressured time in the Jewish home. All the preparations of cleaning, cooking, lighting candles, and keeping food warm need to done before sunset. When darkness falls, these acts are strictly forbidden. So there is only a little time left . . . on all counts:

> . . . and his son Hyrcanus went in to him to remove his tefillin [phylacteries]. But his father rebuked him harshly, and he retreated crestfallen.

"It appears to me," he said to them, "that my father's mind is deranged [*nitrefah*; literally, 'torn']."

But he [R. Eliezer] said to them, "His [Hyrcanus'] mind and his mother's are deranged. How can one neglect a prohibition punishable by stoning, and turn his attention to something only forbidden as a 'shevut'?"

R. Eliezer's son, interestingly, is named after R. Eliezer's father, Hyrcanus. An entire father and son relation is portrayed in these few, but so telling words. They parallel the tense interactions between R. Eliezer and his own father Hyrcanus in the tale of his origins in *Avot de-Rabbi Natan*. Why does Hyrcanus want to remove his father's tefillin? And why does R. Eliezer rebuke him so harshly? Why does he even insist on wearing tefillin at this time? Despite his illness, we see that R. Eliezer is sharp and capable of intense rebuke. Once again, a critical moment in his life is framed by "wounded feelings," as in the story of the oven of Akhnai.

Hyrcanus could be crestfallen due to the severe rebuke, or from his father's ignoring the law of not wearing tefillin on the Sabbath. In other words, his father's refusal to have his tefillin taken off for the Sabbath means he has become deranged. There is an ironic undertow here: after all, the reasoning of R. Eliezer is also questioned in "The Oven of Akhnai" and leads to his banning. The question of whose mind is "*nitrefah*" is at stake in that climactic debate, as well as the issue of whose motives and actions are pure. There too, even though R. Eliezer's reasoning is sharp and he has heavenly aid, he is overruled by a majority on the legal level. That narrative sympathizes with him on an emotional level. He also begins this scene struggling not to be overruled by his son.

Here, the visiting Sages, who negated his judgment before, understand that in this situation, R. Eliezer's behavior and legal reasoning are quite accurate. The prohibition of wearing phylacteries on Shabbat is a rabbinic law.[4] But transgressing the other Sabbath prohibitions of cooking and lighting candles after nightfall—which Hyrcanus and his mother are dangerously delaying to attend to R. Eliezer—is a far worse transgression and entails a much more severe penalty. So, R. Eliezer wins this first battle with his son and the listening Sages by displaying his mental acuity and spiritual fierceness despite his waning physical powers. In essence, this is still the same R. Eliezer as before the ban and his illness.

Hyrcanus might have known the legal issues; perhaps he misreads his father's halakhic argument and response, or just does not grasp the personal side of his father's behavior. Or Hyrcanus could be worried that his father will soon expire. In Jewish law, as we have seen, a dead body is called *avi avot ha-tumah*, the main source of ritual impurity. On the Sabbath, a dead body cannot be moved, nor can tefillin remain on it. Is this the reason for his urgency and worry? In this case, his father would be reacting harshly since he thinks Hyrcanus is trying to "put him in the grave." Here the themes of ritual purity and impurity—and their intimate relation to the very being of R. Eliezer—resurface. The story, I think, is also subtly probing the question: After all is said and done, and after the ban which has itself been a kind of "living death" for him—are R. Eliezer and his teachings "pure"? What would it take for him and his teachings to be accepted again? Moreover, the story also enacts that very process; it does the work of that purification.

The shadow of the banning is present in many other verbal clues in the story. For instance, when Hyrcanus says "It appears to me that my father's mind is deranged," the phrase used in Hebrew for "it appears to me" is *ki-medumeh ani*. It echoes the two times that phrase is used in highly charged moments in the story of the oven of Akhnai. One was when R. Akiva dresses in black and comes to delicately and indirectly inform R. Eliezer of the ban. R. Akiva says, "It appears to me [*ki-medumeh li*] that your colleagues are keeping their distance from you." R. Akiva, the disciple, is a closer "son" to R. Eliezer, far more in tune with him than his biological son, Hyrcanus. Hyrcanus uses the phrase *ki-medumeh ani* out of blank and frantic misunderstanding; R. Akiva uses it with the utmost psychological perception and sympathy.

Later in the story of Akhnai when Rabban Gamaliel—the head of the Sanhedrin (High Court) who approved and carried out the ban—is in danger of drowning in a storm, Rabban Gamaliel says "It appears to me [*ki-medumeh li*] that this is on account of R. Eliezer." So the phrase is used in these three different instances when a character confronts a painful reality associated with separation and death. Yet it is a kind of qualifying phrase— why not just make the statement outright, without the "it appears to me"? Perhaps the phrase rhetorically inserts some doubt in our minds about the ability of the person saying it to fully confront the truth of what he is saying, or some ambivalence on his part. Each instance, as well, involves a problematic but critical decision on an issue of Jewish law. In the story of R. Eliezer's passing, the phrase returns again and underscores the rent between father and son, the alienation of R. Eliezer, and it reminds us of the ban and R. Eliezer's impending rending from the world.[5]

However we may try to understand Hyrcanus, the son's ambiguous motives and reactions help create the dramatic tension of the story. The scene itself is poignant: an ill, old, but still fierce man being treated like an object by his son. As Yonah Fraenkel observes, Hyrcanus seems to think his father is so muddled, he does not even need to be careful. He comments loudly enough so that his father overhears.[6]

Scene 2: Enter Sages; Students and Teachers

> The Sages, seeing that his mind was clear, went into his chamber
> and sat down at a distance of four cubits from him.

The Sages now enter his bedroom for their visit, and our narrator leaves us to wonder what *their* precise motive is. Why did they stay outside his room at first? Are they waiting for him to call them in, for him to recant? Are they first cautiously observing the situation of his health and mind? Have they come only because he is dying, or because they want to test him and see if they can lift the ban, reintegrate him into the community at the last moment? Someone who has been banned would also suffer even after his death—his bier would be stoned.

The story repeats the verb "*nikhnas*" (went in). This phrase contrasts with its opposite—"*yatza*"—especially when R. Eliezer's soul *yatzah* "goes out," leaves him at the moment of his death. This "coming in/going out" verbal pattern enacts the larger themes of acceptance/expulsion that run through all the R. Eliezer stories we have looked at. These themes climax at the moment of his death. Now the Sages move into his intimate space, closer to his bed. This move "inside" breaks a barrier between them; they come into his inner sanctum, but sit at a distance of four cubits. A "cubit" was the distance from the thumb or other finger to the elbow, or about eighteen inches. The laws of the ban required everyone to keep a distance of four cubits from the banned person. Usually, visiting friends of a gravely ill person will come quite close to comfort the sufferer, so here the distance is particularly stinging. This shift in space, in the physical movement of the Sages, also marks a shift in the roles of the characters and their language. The tension continues: What will the interchange be like? Will there be time to lift the ban before he expires? If R. Eliezer's mind has been disturbed, they will not be able to lift the ban at all.

R. Eliezer now moves further from being a passive object to an active inquisitor and speaker. He initiates the conversation: "Why have you come?" The question is pointed and poignant. Would it be said in a tone of bitterness, sadness, skepticism, provocation, curiosity, defensiveness, nostalgia? There is mutual testing. He needs to know their current attitude towards him—and they need to know his attitude towards them since the time after the ban has elapsed. They reply:

> "We have come to study Torah."
> "And why didn't you come before now?" he asked.
> "We had no time," they responded.

What kind of answer is this? Another wounding by words? An impolitic evasion? Certainly not one that would be of much comfort. R. Yosef Hayyim, the Chief Rabbi of Baghdad (1832–1909), known as "Ben Ish Hai," discusses the story in his well-known Talmudic commentary, *Ben Yehoyada*. He attempts to justify their words as heightened sensitivity: they do not want to tell him they have come because he is about to die, nor do they want to refer to the ban.[7] But whatever their motives, this is once again a dialogue of the one versus the many, R. Eliezer versus the Sages. Who will outweigh whom this time?

According to laws of banning—*niddui*—one is allowed to learn Torah from someone who has been banned. If so, they could have come before and R. Eliezer's second question is even more painful. If, as some other rabbinic commentators argue, R. Eliezer was not banned but excommunicated, they would *not* have been allowed to study Torah from him. If the latter is the case, then his question "And why didn't you come before?" might express his continued bitterness at the Sages' refusal to acknowledge his interpretive system as legitimate. It would voice his lack of regret at opposing them at all costs and his continued belief in the truth of what he had said, notwithstanding the continued personal injury. The dramatic construction of the scene, though, seems to me to indicate his having been banned, not excommunicated—especially since in the Jerusalem Talmud the scene is placed in the context of laws of banning and mourning.[8] In either case, his bitterness, anguish, and recalcitrance are strong. If the Sages have come to test him in order to remove either the excommunication or the ban, they will now need to discourse about Torah with him. They face a formidable opponent.

"We had no time," was their answer. To this he responds with a shocking, abrupt statement breaking the pace, rhythm, and nature of the first interchange: "He then said, 'I will be surprised if these die a natural death.'" This could be another sign of the lingering wound from his banning, or a frustrated response to their feeble and humiliating answer, or his pondering a larger logic of cause and effect. In "The Oven of Akhnai" story, the oceans threatened to drown Rabban Gamaliel because he had approved and executed the ban on R. Eliezer—even though Rabban Gamaliel claimed he had done so out of pure motives to protect the Torah from becoming factionalized. Will those other Sages, who opposed him and tacitly agreed with the ban also inevitably bring disaster upon themselves? Or, as some classical rabbinic commentators would like to argue, are his words not about his personal injury but about the injury done to the Torah itself? They did not come to study Torah with him, and so a great deal of his precious knowledge will be lost forever after his impending demise. Nor did they perform the duty of "attending upon him" (*shimmush hakhamim*; *Berakhot* 7b), visiting him to learn from his personal presence and assisting him with his needs. If they have cut themselves off from that ultimate source of life—Torah—and injured the Torah—their death, too, could not be natural.

The "camera's focus" now moves in for a close-up of the dialogue between R. Eliezer and R. Akiva:

> R. Akiva asked him, "And what will mine be?"
> "Yours will be crueler than theirs," he answered.

The conversation is set during the time of the brutal Roman occupation in which many of the Sages were cruelly tortured to death for continuing to teach Torah. The persecution by the emperor Hadrian was especially intense after the Bar Kokhba rebellion in 132 CE. The Talmud portrays R. Akiva as initially a supporter of Bar Kokhba, who many believed was the Messiah due to his military successes, until Bar Kokhba's disastrous end at Bethar (Jerusalem Talmud, *Ta'anit* 4). Akiva's death as a martyr was one of the worst described in *Berakhot* 61b, his flesh torn apart by iron combs. In a sense, R. Akiva was later also "banned"—the Romans had forbidden the teaching of Torah, but he resisted and was put to death for it.[9]

The exchange between him and R. Eliezer here is especially terse and even more so in Hebrew. It would literally translate:

"Mine—what is it?"
"Yours—worse than theirs."

In Hebrew, the possessives "mine,""yours," "theirs" all share the same prepositional root, *shel* meaning "of" or "belonging to." It is then inflected with slightly different suffixes: *sheli* literally means "of me"; *shelkha* means "of you"; *shelahen* translates "of them." So the sound of the dialogue between R. Elieizer and R. Akiva in Hebrew is even more terse, repetitive, and raw:

Sheli, mah hu?
Shelkha kashah mi-shelahen.

Intimate interlocutors only need minimal words to understand each other. The close repetition of the Hebrew sounds in this piece of dialogue and the way the lines mirror each other, subtly underscores the persisting intimate relation between the teacher and his outstanding student, even amidst all the pain. But after such an answer, what can there be left to say? We will not hear any more direct words from R. Akiva until his agonized emotional outburst at R. Eliezer's funeral at the story's end. R. Eliyahu Henkin speculates that R. Akiva's anguished words at R. Eliezer's funeral and his beating of his own flesh till blood flows into the earth express his bitter remorse and belated recognition that R. Eliezer had been correct in his estimation not to support further political rebellion.[10] Much blood flowed into the ground from that failed revolt, the nation was decimated, and countless Jews were sold into slavery.

But their tense interchange in our story leaves room for many questions. Why will R. Akiva's death be worse? Because he was a close student, the greatest student, had the most "open heart," and still neglected coming to study with or attend R. Eliezer? Because the story is being written and edited later (after the terrible consequences of the Bar Kokhba rebellion), and Akiva's martyrdom is already known and needs to be explained through a new, more quietist ideology?[11] We can play with many interpretive possibilities, but neither R. Eliezer nor the narrator specifies a reason. There is no simple cause-and-effect logic running through this story's web of human reactions, interactions, personal, religious, and political conflicts.

Like all great stories, it is deeper than its manifest content; its blank spaces and silences are as pregnant with meaning as its verbal surfaces. Robert Alter's characterization of biblical narrative also fits this rabbinic tale well:

> An essential aim of the innovative technique of fiction worked out by the ancient Hebrew writers was to produce a certain indeterminacy of meaning, especially in regard to motive, moral character, and psychology . . . . Meaning, perhaps for the first time in narrative literature, was conceived as a *process*, requiring continual revision . . . continual suspension of judgment, weighing of multiple possibilities, brooding over gaps in the information provided.[12]

That indeed also well describes my process in this book: continual revision, brooding over gaps, and offering multiple possibilities. Alter argues that in biblical narrative, this formal indeterminacy expresses a paradoxical Jewish theology which juxtaposes the controlling providence of an ultimately unknowable but ethical God and the freedom God gives to humans to struggle with their destiny through their acts and words. The divine/human intersection in our Talmudic story is an equally complex knot, like the ties of the tefillin R. Eliezer is wearing. Divine causality does not work here in simple, linear manipulable ways. Perhaps that is one reason the context of the story is a discussion of sorcery. For sorcery, in part, is the human attempt to manipulate and control the divine—to cut through those difficult knots in our lives, to deal with the dark spaces, fabricate mechanical actions to coerce the divine will. Or at least to make it appear to be so and profit from the possibility.

Tefillin, with their sets of knots and straps which wrap around the arm and head of the wearer, express the binding of human mind and action to God in a personal and intimate mutual relation. Even God, the Talmud says in a bold midrash, "puts on tefillin" (*Berakhot* 6a). So this visual image of R. Eliezer wrapped in tefillin as he speaks with his visitors on his death bed reinforces his purity, his attachment to heaven, despite his irascibility in the scene.

Could there be another connection to sorcery in the way the Sages have failed to come and attend upon him? The Talmud in *Sotah* 22a discusses all kinds of "pious fools." On the list is "one who learned Scripture and Mishnah but did not attend upon the Sages":

If one has learned Scripture and Mishnah but did not attend upon the Sages, R. Eleazar says he is an *am ha-aretz* [ignoramus]. R. Shemuel bar Nahmani says he is a boor. R. Yannai says he is a Samaritan. R. Aha bar Ya'akov says he is a magician. R. Nahman bar Yitzhak said: "R. Aha bar Ya'akov's definition is the one most likely correct, because as the popular saying goes, 'The magician mumbles and knows not what he says; the *tanna* [teacher] recites and knows not what he says.'"

There is a kind of ironic wink and jest in these lines, I think, and jab at certain kinds of pedagogues and scholars. To "attend upon the Sages" implies a deep personal connection. One can amass textual knowledge, but without that personal connection to the teacher, without the absorption of the teacher's way of learning and unique traditions—and especially without emulating his or her way of embodying what is taught, then one is not only ignorant but a sorcerer! One just mumbles magic words, produces some dazzling temporary effects, and the student is duped. We all have had teachers like this, I suspect, and know the unfortunate students and would be scholars who imitate this magical mumbling.[13]

R. Jeffrey Saks perceptively adds another way to explain "illusion" in the context of the story:

> The students come at the end with their "excuses"—we didn't have time before. Life is like that: our little white lies and social niceties are a type of "illusion"; like the man who pulls a rabbit out of the hat, or saws the pretty girl in half. We know it's not real; it's just an illusion, but we suspend our sense of critical thinking in order to enjoy the show. R. Eliezer won't go along with the illusion they try to create in the end. He knows why they've stayed away.[14]

Scene 3: The Body as Torah Scroll Closing Up, and the Pathos of Teaching

> He then took his two arms and placed them over his heart, and said: "Woe to you, two arms of mine, which are like two Scrolls of the Torah being rolled up."

In part three of the story, R. Eliezer "opens," gives a long dramatic monologue and gestures with his body in powerful show of "visual rhetoric." Arms are symbols of power, of reaching and grasping high. In the Jewish mystical tradition's mapping of the body, the arm corresponds to the ability to reach supernal levels of understanding, since it is the one part of the body which can literally reach above the head, "higher than intellect." Now, however, all is closing up. R. Eliezer's power of teaching—his "arm"—was diminished by the ban and is soon to be cut off by death. It is as if he is drawing his arms into position for burial and also "cradling a Torah scroll close to his heart." He covers his heart with his hands. Some commentators interpret this gesture to signify the wound to his heart. Ben Ish Hai, characteristically, sees in it a mute cry that all his "wars of Torah," all the halakhic debates in which he engaged, were from a pure heart, with pure intentions, "for the sake of heaven."[15] This powerful image of arms covering his heart "like two Scrolls of the Torah rolling up" is also a final and total embrace of Torah as he is dying. He becomes the Torah, an "embodied Torah," the ultimate identity of a rabbinic Sage. That gesture and the work of this story itself begin to insert him back into the tradition, to "remove the ban," and place him firmly at the "heart" of the Torah itself.[16]

Nevertheless, there is pathos and an uneasy undercurrent in these words and images. For these are also the thin arms of a sick elderly man. And this is a closed-up Torah, one whose letters are not visible and can't be read. How hard it had been for R. Yohanan ben Zakkai to "open" him, open the mouth of the young R. Eliezer, but now all is being closed again. The "plastered cistern" is being sealed. Although he has visitors, his former dear colleagues and closest student, at his bedside in these final moments, his words and gestures convey a sense of aloneness.

In "The Oven of Akhnai" story, R. Akiva had dressed in black as a sign of mourning to inform R. Eliezer of the ban, hinting it to him as if sharing his fate. At the end of this story, R Akiva also takes his arm to his chest, beating his heart till the blood flows in mourning and anguish for the loss of R. Eliezer and his Torah, and perhaps guilt. These gestures all signify a meaning to the story beyond its literal words—the two hearts, of student and teacher, are intertwined in Torah in love, in pain, and in destiny. There is an unspoken intimacy between the student and teacher here, expressible only through hints and gestures . . . as in so many of the deepest relationships. The gestures and the metaphors used in all the stories we've looked at function like a kind of musical counterpoint to the words. As with a film's soundtrack, they give resonances to the words beyond their denotative meanings and allow for the coexistence of contradictory feelings and meanings.

R. Eliezer now speaks of his life as a teacher and student:

> Much Torah I learned, and much Torah I taught. Much Torah I
> learned, but I did not even skim [*hesarti*] from my teachers as much
> as a dog licks from the sea. Much Torah I taught, but my disciples only
> drew from me as much as a painting stick from its tube.[17]

Levinas notes that in R. Eliezer's description of his relation to his teachers, "The master is someone's disciple. He has a feeling of guilt towards
his masters. He too did not know how to take what they were offering."[18]
If this reading is correct, we are witnessing the remarkable confession of a
master teacher and scholar—itself a final act of great teaching. But are not
all students ultimately in this position? Only after the passing of our great
teachers (or of anyone), do we realize we never knew how to fully take what
they were offering. Are we responsible for that? Is part of the pathos here
the cruel impossibility of never being able to drink fully of their wisdom
or love?

For what is that powerful metaphor of the dog licking from the sea? Why
the difference between the images R. Eliezer employs for himself and the
one he uses to describe his students—the stick dipping into a narrow tube
(probably a tube of medication or eye cosmetic). A dog, out of mad thirst
or desire, might try to lick the sea for its salt-taste, or become entranced
by the waves. But there is also something uncomfortable and harsh in
that image of that dog. Especially since dogs were not viewed in Talmudic
times in the affectionate way we moderns relate to them. There is a kind of
severe, demanding judgment involved in the comparison, characteristic of
the temperament of R. Eliezer. That oral image is reminiscent of the young
Eliezer in the story of his beginnings, so hungry to study that he ate dirt.
From a literary point of view, all these oral images are well suited to char-
acterize one who will become a great teacher of the Oral Torah. Here, at the
end of his life, his thirst to learn and teach remains unquenched, despite
all the ways in which he was the "plastered cistern" filled with knowledge.
However much a cistern holds, it is nothing compared to the vastness, the
endlessness of the ocean. However much water is drawn from the ocean,
it is not diminished. And if one licks the sea waters, one becomes only
thirstier.[19] Moreover, drinking signifies imbibing and therefore absorbing
deeply and internally; painting, on the other hand, is an external application and here merely decorative.

Ben Ish Hai offers an alternate and rather ingenious reading. The metaphors, he thinks, signify two different perspectives: from R. Eliezer's perspective, *his* own teachers were a vast sea; but from his students' perspective, their teacher R. Eliezer held only a contained measure, a small tube—and that is why they did not come to learn from him. A dog runs all day from place to place to find food, he observes, and so R. Eliezer "ran" to study Torah from his teachers. His students, though, stayed in one place; they did not run after him. That type of learning is inert. Like the paintbrush, unless someone picks it up and inserts it in the tube to absorb color, it is lifeless and uncreative. "I have learned much from my teachers, more from my colleagues, but from my students most of all" (*Ta'anit* 7a) proclaims a well-known Talmudic passage. Ben Ish Hai applies this famous rabbinic saying to the metaphors here: if R. Eliezer assiduously studied with and attended upon his teachers, then his teachers increased their wisdom; they attained more from the process than he did from them. In that case, he did not diminish the ratio of his learning to theirs at all, because as much as he learned from them, they kept learning even more in the process! But R. Eliezer's own students, who separated from him, just "dipped the paintbrush in the tube"; they learned from him in an irregular way, not assiduously, and did not grow personally attached to him. So he did not gain wisdom from them.

Some might find Ben Ish Hai's interpretations of the story to be overly pietistic. But he spurs us to take seriously the meaning of these metaphors. Indeed, from a literary point of view, the tube as a small closed container holding in precious oils echoes and reverses the plastered cistern image used to describe R. Eliezer by his own teacher, R. Yohanan ben Zakkai. The tube of paint is much diminished in size and constricted; only a small stick can take out dabs of it. In the monologue we are given here, the metaphors used to express his relations to his own students and teachers create meanings in many ways and on many levels. Yet there is a coherent underground network of associations in all three stories we've looked at. These covert associations, I suggest, are part of the texts' sophisticated pedagogical strategies.

SORCERY: "THE USES OF ENCHANTMENT"

As the story now continues, we seem to fall through a looking-glass when R. Eliezer's monologue suddenly drops us into fields of magic cucumbers, and he reminisces about another intimate encounter with his close student R. Akiva and all that was left untaught.

> Not only that, I have studied three hundred laws on the subject of a deep bright spot, and no one has ever asked me anything about them. And I have studied three hundred—or, as others state, three thousand laws—about the planting of cucumbers [by magic], and no one ever asked me about them except Akiva ben Yosef.
>
> Once he and I were walking together on a road, when he said to me, "My Teacher, teach me about the planting of cucumbers." I said something, and the whole field [about us] was filled with cucumbers. Then he said: "Teacher, you taught me how to plant them. Now teach me how to uproot them." I said something, and all the cucumbers were gathered in one place.

There are technical issues here with which we need not become overly involved. But in brief, the biblical law of the "deep bright spot" has to do with signs of leprosy (Lev. 13:2) and their relation to ritual purity and impurity. Creating cucumbers through sorcery links the story back to its context in tractate *Sanhedrin*, which had been analyzing the uses and punishments for such practices before it so startlingly swept us into R. Eliezer's deathbed scene. By now, we have almost forgotten that the oral law with which our entire story began stipulated that a sorcerer is subject to penalty if he actually performs the act, but *not* if he only creates illusions. He would be liable if he would create the cucumbers "for profit," but not if he only made them just seem to magically appear. It's an interesting but perplexing distinction.

What is this all about? Levinas, tongue-in-cheek, observes that the sorcerer here is not very demanding, but a poor one who just produces an inexpensive product—cucumbers in a field.

> To stay at the level of illusion does not have great consequences, but if the sorcerer *picks* the cucumbers, if the illusion manages to fit itself within an economic process—and modern economic life is, after all, the place of preference for the harvesting of illusory cucumbers and for the heavy profits attached to such a harvest, sorcery becomes a criminal act.[20]

Levinas is ironically reading this passage as an apt description of modern capitalist economies which often depend on selling "illusions," that is, "magically" making objects seem far more valuable than they really are and harvesting immense profits from that kind of "sorcery."

The Babylonian Talmud's editorial decision to insert the story of R. Eliezer's passing into a discussion of sorcery prods me to ponder further the relation of sorcery to death. Death is the ultimate experience we would all like to "trick"—to magically control or reverse. In a way, all other forms of sorcery could be seen as subsets of that: panicked attempts to control the mysterious forces of life and death which assail us in arbitrary and cruel ways. In Michael Chabon's poignant novel, *The Amazing Adventures of Kavalier & Clay*, whose plot revolves around the relations between magic, Jews, the history of comics, and the Holocaust, the main character Joe Kavalier comes to see death as the ultimate magician:

> He began to understand, after all those years of study and perfor-
> mance, of feats and wonders and surprises, the nature of magic. The
> magician seems to promise that something torn to bits might be
> mended without a seam, that what had vanished might reappear, that
> a scattered handful of doves or dust might be reunited by a word, that
> a paper rose consumed by fire could be made to bloom from a pile of
> ash. But everyone knew that it was only an illusion. The true magic of
> this broken world lay in the ability of the things it contained to vanish,
> to become so thoroughly lost, that they might never have existed in
> the first place.[21]

In other words, the magician promises that our broken world and our losses can be restored with just a word, a blink of an eye. He or she touches on the deep aches of our inevitable losses. Joe Kavalier's rueful reflections here locate death as the "true magic" since it makes things vanish so thoroughly that "they might have never existed in the first place." Magic is not the counterforce of death, then, but implicated in it. Yet in Jewish law, as we noted in "The Oven of Akhnai" story, death is the *avi avot tumah*, the principal source of ritual impurity. If Freud is correct and there is a "death instinct" (*thanatos*) opposing a "life instinct" (*eros*) in the human psyche, then making death the source of ritual impurity would inhibit an unhealthy religious-aesthetic fascination with death. In Hamlet's famous words, it is not to be "a consummation devoutly to be wished"—neither an object of sacred longing, nor of sacred terror. R. Joseph B. Soloveitchik movingly describes how Jewish law tries to vanquish even the fear of death by transforming this phenomenon, which subjectively so terrifies us, into an object of human observation and cognition. He relates a story of his famous grandfather, R. Hayyim of Brisk, a Talmudic genius. When the fear of death would seize him,

> he would throw himself with his entire heart and mind, into the study
> of the laws of tents and corpse defilement. And these laws, which
> revolve about such difficult and complex problems as defilement of the
> grave, defilement of a tent . . . a vessel with a tight fitting cover upon it
> in a tent in which a corpse lies, etc. etc. would calm the turbulence of
> his soul and would imbue it with the spirit of joy and gladness. When
> halakhic man fears death, his sole weapon wherewith to fight this
> terrible dread is the eternal law of the *Halakhah*. The act of objectifica-
> tion triumphs over the subjective terror of death.[22]

Such sublimation may indeed work for a brilliant legal master, but is far less available for the average person, for whom those terrors are so powerful and for whom "magic" in all its forms is so tempting, even in what appears to be our contemporary, desacralized, and secular world.

Levinas also asks about the relation of sorcery to ritual purity and impurity in our story. What indeed, he asks, was this entire project of the Pharisees—the rabbinic party to whom R. Eliezer and his colleagues belonged? The word "Pharisees" comes from the Hebrew word "*perushim*," literally meaning "those who separated." It also connects to the word for "holy" (*kadosh*), in its sense of being "set apart." What were the Pharisees "separating" from and what were they trying to accomplish by constructing this system of ritual purity and impurity, defending and elaborating it even after the destruction of the Temple, when it had lost most of its practical applicability? His commentary on this text was given in the context of a colloquium on "The Jews in a Desacralized Society" in 1971 and, though somewhat difficult, is worth exploring further for the broader philosophi-cal insights he gives to the story. In tying his commentary to the topic of the colloquium, Levinas prefaces his remarks by saying:

> I have always asked myself if holiness, that is, separation or purity,
> the essence without admixture that can be called Spirit and which
> animates the Jewish tradition—or to which Jewish tradition aspires—

can dwell in a world that has not been desacralized. I have asked myself—and that is the real question—whether the world is sufficiently desacralized to receive such purity. The sacred is in fact the half-light in which the sorcery the Jewish tradition abhors flourishes. The "other side," the reverse or obverse of the Real, Nothingness condensed to Mystery . . . . Sorcery, first cousin, perhaps even sister, of the sacred, is the mistress of appearance.[23]

He further comments in a complex paragraph:

The sacred which degenerates is worse than the sacred which disappears . . . . [In the pharisaic project] we find [a] separation from a world in which *appearance* falsifies *that which appears* . . . in which desacralization is nothing but a new magic, augmenting the sacred, its degeneration into sorcery being one with its generation. In this bewitched world . . . the *separation* of the Pharisees is put into practice. It is an absence from the immediacy of possessing, by means of prohibitions and rules, a hope of *holiness* in the space of a *sacred* that cannot be purified, *Judaism as an irreducible modality of being present to the world* . . . . The sacred which degenerates is worse than the sacred which disappears.[24]

The quotation is rather opaque, but in essence, I think Levinas is here interpreting the story with a special sensitivity to the malaise of modern society due also to his experiences in World War II as a French Jew caught up in the Holocaust, and his own teacher, the philosopher Martin Heidegger, having becoming a Nazi. He wants to make a sharp distinction here between a type of Jewish "holiness" and a degenerate "sacred"; he sees the Rabbis' project as an attempt to bring "holiness" (*kedushah*) into a world where the "sacred" had become a degenerate form of mystification and violence. In the modern world, Nazi ideology used and abused sentiments of "the sacred" in highly effective and terrifying ways. Desacralization is also the modern intellectual attempt since the Enlightenment to purify the "sacred," either by expunging it or replacing it with secular ideologies that purport to be rational, critical and "demystifying." But, he is suggesting, these attempts nevertheless also slide into forms of sorcery:

That is what sorcery is: the modern world: nothing is identical to itself;

no one is identical to himself; nothing gets said for no word has its own meaning; all speech is a magical whisper; no one listens to what you say; everyone suspects behind your words a not-said, a conditioning, an ideology.[25]

This is an implicit critique of various philosophical tendencies in modern and postmodern thought, especially Marxism, Freudianism, Deconstruction and their offspring. All roughly share the assumption that nothing is as it appears, nothing is identical to itself, and that behind everything that is said lies a suspicious ideology.

Levinas' own intellectual project was to try to halt the degeneration and violence rooted in so much of Western culture through a radical philosophical rethinking of ethics, one inspired by Jewish sources. For him, the pharisaic construction of laws of ritual purity and impurity is a paradigmatic ethical move. It is a way of removing a person from "the immediacy of possessing"—by which he means the violence inherent in the egoistic desire to immediately grasp, possess, and control objects and persons in the world (even if it be as subtle as a philosopher's desire to totally grasp the world through abstract systems of thought). The pharisaic "separation" was an attempt, by contrast, to intervene in those modes of violent "being and having"—however gross or subtle they may be—and engender "holiness in the world," and thus oppose "sacred" sorcery.[26]

R. Askénazi, whom I also have quoted at length in these pages, was Levinas' colleague in Paris after World War II. Both had personally suffered in the Nazi period. Both later struggled philosophically with the problem of violence in Western culture and attempted to reconstruct Jewish thought and community in France. R. Askénazi alternatively describes the Pharisees not as exemplars of a Levinasian philosophical form of ethics, nor as the strict, dry, legalists portrayed in Christian polemics, but as those who were faithfully trying to find a way to continue the knowledge given previously via direct revelation to the Hebrew prophets. The Pharisees, that is, were the real inheritors and continuers of the *prophetic* tradition . . . *after* prophecy ceases and the Temple is destroyed. For the Pharisees, this entailed continuing the Hebraic and national political option as opposed to the views of the competing contemporary sects of Sadducees, Essenes, and Christians. The Sadducees advocated assimilation and Hellenization; the Essenes developed an intense monastic asceticism. The Zealots, whom we encountered in the story of R. Yohanan ben Zakkai's escape from besieged

Jerusalem, were the radical political rebels, but disappeared after failing to prevent the destruction of the Temple and the Romans' brutal suppression of their rebellion. As R. Askénazi also notes, for the Pharisees, continued debate and application of the Temple laws and system of purity and impurity where possible, now also transform the kohen, the Temple priest (who was intimately involved in laws of purity in his service), into the model for every Jew *after* the Temple's destruction. *Perushim*, the Hebrew term for Pharisees, is the Talmudic translation of the word for *kadosh*, "holy."[27]

Levinas and R. Askénazi's reflections on the meaning of the Pharasaic revolution are profound, but we are still left to ponder why our story connects R. Eliezer's passing with its discussion of the laws of purity and impurity with sorcery. There is indeed an enduring and ineradicable human fascination with magic and sorcery, as Harry Potter's recent success attests. Joe Kavalier, Michael Chabon's central character in *The Amazing Adventures of Kavalier & Clay*, once again reflects with great insight on the source of that fascination, when he ties it to another famous legend of rabbinic magic: the story of the Golem, an animated being created from inanimate matter by Maharal, R. Yehudah Loew of Prague, in the sixteenth century to protect the Jews of that city.

> Each in his own way, attempted to fashion their various golems . . .
> [The] shaping of a golem, to him, was a gesture of hope, offered against
> hope, in a time of desperation. It was the expression of yearning that
> a few magic words and artful hand might produce something—one
> poor, dumb powerful thing—exempt from the crushing strictures,
> from the ills, cruelties and inevitable failures of the greater Creation.
> It was the voicing of a vain wish, when you got down to it, to escape
> . . . if only for one instant; to poke his head through the borders of this
> world, with its harsh physics, into the mysterious spirit worlds that lay
> beyond.[28]

"Hope against hope in a time of desperation" is a phrase that well characterizes R. Eliezer's teacher, R. Yohanan ben Zakkai, the great Pharisee, as he "escaped" from Jerusalem to save Judaism in Yavneh. And it also aptly describes the religious and political project of the students and colleagues who succeeded him, among them R. Eliezer, R. Yehoshua, and R. Akiva. Their teachings ensured the survival, life, and growth of the Jewish people and Torah for the next 2000 years—a form of "magic," in its own right.

These Rabbis also engaged in other forms of practical magic as we see in our story. Before we return to those magic cucumbers in the story of R. Eliezer's passing, let's ask a radical question: what, indeed, is the difference between the laws of purity and impurity and sorcery itself? How can something magically become pure once it has been impure just from sprinkling the ashes of a red cow upon it, or breaking and reconstructing it (like the oven), or immersing it in water? In a daring midrash on chapter 19 of the biblical book of Numbers, the Sages themselves boldly ask this question, probing how close their own system of purity and impurity is to magic. Numbers 19 contains key laws about ritual impurity and describes various forms of purification through immersion in water and the ashes of the "red heifer." In this midrashic story commenting on that chapter, an idolater comes to R. Yohanan ben Zakkai and challenges him:

> "These rites that you perform look like a kind of witchcraft. You bring a heifer, burn it, pound it, and take its ashes. If one of you is made impure by a dead body, you sprinkle upon him two or three drops and you say to him: 'You are pure.'"
>
> R. Yohanan asked him: "Has the demon of madness ever possessed you?"
>
> "No," he replied.
>
> "Have you ever seen a man possessed by this demon of madness?"
>
> "Yes," said he.
>
> "And what do you do in such a case?"
>
> "We bring roots," he replied, "and make them smoke under him, then we sprinkle water upon the demon and it flees."
>
> Said R. Yohanan to him: "Let your ears hear what you utter with your mouth! Precisely so is this spirit a spirit of impurity as it is written, 'And also I will cause the prophets and the spirit of impurity to pass out of the land' [Zech. 13:2]. Water of purification is sprinkled upon the impure and the spirit flees."

After the idolater leaves, R. Yohanan's disciples demand a better explanation. To them, he speaks on an entirely different level subtly deconstructing the literal reading of the biblical text:

Said R. Yohanan to them: "By your life! It is not the dead that makes impure or the water that purifies! The Holy One, blessed be He, merely says: 'I have laid down a statute, I have issued a decree. You are not allowed to transgress My decree.' As it is written, 'This is the statute of the Torah [*zot hukkat ha-Torah*].' [Num. 19:1]" (*Numbers Rabbah* 19:8)

One might view R. Yohanan's statement as an attempt to inculcate blind obedience to authority. As Simi Peters argues, however, he is warning his disciples to not think magically—especially about these rites and the biblical text. In other words: be careful not to believe that there is any inherent "impurity" in these objects or in the natural world, or any magic power in the water that purifies. In philosophical terms we would put it this way: the system is "arbitrary" not "ontological." But it is a system of rules given by God, subject to human application and reasoning in the Oral Law. In Peters' felicitous formulation, magic "assigns meanings where they do not belong"; it projects onto reality a false appearance; "magic is seeing in something what it is not."[29]

This insight would connect us back to "The Oven of Akhnai" debate and R. Yehoshua's proclamation that the Torah "is not in heaven" but decided according to the majority. Absolute truth, in this view, would not inhere in these laws—even if Heaven agreed with R. Eliezer, even if he could make nature magically support his position in the debate by various miracles, and even if he had the purest intentions. Could that be another source of God's smiling: "My sons have defeated me, My sons have defeated me"? We smile and laugh when we see something from another perspective. Dogmatists do not smile when "defeated"; there is only one perspective, one meaning, and it is absolute, "sacred," and inevitably degenerates into violence. The contemporary rhetorical theorist, Kenneth Burke, well understood the meaning of the "comic perspective," especially in fighting forms of dogmatism and embodying a dialectic of incompatible opposites. There is often an underlying comic, ironic tone in many midrashic stories, and certainly here in R. Yohanan's dialogue with the idolaters.[30] The smiling rabbinic God of the Akhnai story also engages in a generative and reciprocal relation to the Rabbis and Jewish people, to the extent of even studying the Torah and citing decisions in the name of the Sages! This same midrashic commentary, *Midrash Rabbah*, Num. 19:7, also connects R. Eliezer ben Hyrcanus to the deep secret of laws about the Red Heifer, whose ashes purify someone who has been in contact with a dead body—which is the prime source of *tumah*. God is portrayed as studying these difficult and perplexing laws and quoting interpretations in the name of R. Eliezer himself.

A REPLAY OF THE OVEN OF AKHNAI

After R. Eliezer recounts his journey with R. Akiva in the fields of magic cucumbers, the tempo of the narrative suddenly changes. The scene shifts back to the Sages, who rapidly interrogate R. Eliezer with a series of question about down-to-earth practical laws of *tumah* and *taharah*, ritual purity and impurity. This is a replay of issues which caused his banning. Is he now willing to recant? One senses their urgency in the face of his previous speech and his impending death in the abrupt terseness of their questions:

> They said to him: "A ball, a shoe-form, an amulet, a pearl-pouch, a small weight—what is the law?"

These various cases are old questions he and they have disputed before. Ben Ish Hai senses rhetorical subtlety here and interprets their line of questioning as a hint to R. Eliezer why they did not previously come to visit him. That is, they are indirectly answering his rebuke by alluding to the debate over the oven of Akhnai. Perhaps they mention cases very closely related to give him a chance to diplomatically alter his opinion, and thus remove the ban.

We need briefly to clarify one technical level of the discussion to grasp the import of this seemingly arcane interchange. Each object the Sages question R. Eliezer about shares this: they all have a sealed leather casing, enclosing some stuffing and sown together with a seam. The ball, for example, is a leather skin stuffed with lamb's wool. They are asking him: (1) Are these objects susceptible to *tumah*, ritual impurity? (2) If they tear open and contract *tumah*, can they be purified by ritual immersion in water just as they are, without removing the inside matter? (3) Does the inside matter become *tame'* (impure) as well—that is, does it constitute an interference to the purification process (which would invalidate it) and therefore need to be removed before immersion, or not?[31] His answer: "*hen teme'in ve-taharatan be-mah she-hen.*" In other words:

"They are *tame'* [susceptible to becoming impure], [and if impure] they are restored to their purity [*taharah*] just as they are."

The English translation makes the sentence much longer and more involved than the compact Hebrew, which intensifies the terse rhythm of the dialogue. Answer: R. Eliezer adheres firmly here to his previous opinions.

The technical issue is whether these objects are complete receptacles. We remember in "The Oven of Akhnai" that only a complete and whole vessel can contract ritual impurity. So if these objects have a hollow inside, that would define them as receptacles, and they *could* contract *tumah* (*Kelim* 2:1). But they are also sewn together . . . is that a permanent closure or not? And then, what if they tear? The majority opinion of the Sages was that sewing them closed still does not make them a receptacle. But what's really at stake here? I would suggest that on another level, the questions themselves are trying to "make torn things whole"—mend the rent between R. Eliezer and his colleagues, his Torah and theirs, earth and heaven, the natural and the divine orders." Once again Michael Chabon puts it so well:

> The magician seems to promise that something torn to bits might be mended without a seam, that what had vanished might reappear, that a scattered handful of doves or dust might be reunited by a word, that a paper rose consumed by fire could be made to bloom from a pile of ash.[32]

But there will be no quick magic here; instead, an arduous intellectual, ethical, and spiritual process must be endured. In short, R. Eliezer himself is the object undergoing "purification" in this scene. Can he be purified "just as he is"?

In the legal case in question here, one cannot break the object to purify it as with the Akhnai oven; it is already torn and needs to be immersed in special waters. But does one have to also remove the inside stuffing for the purification process? R. Eliezer is indeed a vessel that has been "torn," made "impure" by the ban—ironically even his son Hyrcanus says, "I fear my father's mind is *nitrefah*," literally "torn." But as Ora Wiskind-Elper comments, R. Eliezer's "'stuffing'—his personal Torah—is an integral part of him, sewn in and together with his 'outside.' You can't take him apart and purify his parts separately."[33] He was the plastered cistern, the one who had hollowed himself out to fill himself with Torah. The inside stuffing and the outside receptacle are one unit; they must be purified just as they are. In other words, the Sages cannot purify him by breaking him apart—having him disavow his previous halakhic opinions. Unlike a sorcerer, his reality and his appearance are one; his inside and outside are indivisible.[34]

THE FINAL MOMENT: "HOW DOES ONE DIE PROCLAIMING THE RITUAL PURITY OF A SHOE?"

The final question the Sages put to R. Eliezer concerns the status of a shoe on the shoe-form (also technically known as a "last" in English). The cobbler has finished the shoe, but not yet removed it from the shoe-form.

> "What of a shoe that is on the shoe-form?"
> He replied, "*Tahor*" . . . and his soul departed "*be-taharah* [in purity]."

Why are they asking R. Eliezer *this* question as he breathes his last? Where is the broad, wise, philosophical discussion comparable to Plato's famous description of Socrates' dialogue with his students in the *Phaedo* when Socrates is about to drink the hemlock and die? Or as Levinas puts it: "How does one die proclaiming the ritual purity of a shoe?" But indeed, R. Eliezer is like the shoe: his life is about to be completed, his soul is about to be removed from its platform, the body, and taken away. The editors, I believe, have carefully composed the story: the question is not only put *to* R. Eliezer, but it is *about* R. Eliezer himself, and the student reading the text thus *performs* the "purification" process along with the Sages, as R. Eliezer breathes his last.[35]

Beneath the technical legal argument is a conceptual analysis of the creative process, of beginnings and endings, and of the definition of wholeness. It's not done through Greek philosophical speculation, but through precise analysis of a concrete legal case, dealing with a seemingly mundane artifact: the shoe. When indeed does anything really begin, and when is it finally completed? In the case in question, the shoe-form the shoemaker used to create the shoe is made of stuffed leather. Now, is a shoe in this condition—the work on it having been completed, but still sitting on the shoe-form—a finished object or not? It is a borderline case; R. Eliezer debates the shoe question with the Sages in the Mishnah *Kelim* 26:4. His position is that the shoe is not finished until it is actually taken *off* the shoe-form. Only then can the shoe be considered a complete vessel and thus susceptible to *tumah*. While still sitting on the form, it is not finished and can't acquire *tumah*, and therefore it is pure (like his decision on the oven of Akhnai). But the Sages argue the opposite: since the actual work of creating the shoe has been finished, for all practical purposes, it is complete and therefore susceptible to *tumah*. No skilled work is needed to remove it from the shoe-form. And this is also the question about R. Eliezer, who is finishing his life and work and is soon to be removed from this world: Is he pure or not?

The impending end of his life is dramatically portrayed in the image of him as a closing holy Torah scroll. It is now intensified by his final word, a word of halakhic decision: "*tahor*." The effect is heightened because grammatically we can read the word "*be-taharah*" in two ways in the line "and his soul departed *be-taharah*": (1) "His soul departed in purity"—as an adverb, or (2) "his soul departed with purity"—"purity" as a noun, as his final word, his halakhic judgment. This double meaning signifies, I think, that the shoe is *tahor*, and R. Eliezer and his Torah are also pure. In a sense, here he also has the "last word" in the debate about the oven of Akhnai: *tahor*!

But this purity was perhaps too much for this world. Only just after his passing does R. Yehoshua announce the revocation of the ban: "The vow is annulled, the vow is annulled!" *After* his passing, but not before. This cry reinforces our sense that the last word R. Eliezer says about the shoe—is really also about *him*. For someone who is a "living Torah," and whose body merges with the Scroll, these legal issues are indeed inseparable from the essence of his being.

From a literary point of view, the way these objects in the story function—the oven, the ball, the shoe—reminds me of the poet T.S. Eliot's famous term, "objective correlative." Eliot, in his classic 1919 essay, "Hamlet and His Problems," reacted against the Romantic concept of poetry as the "powerful overflow of spontaneous feelings"—Wordsworth's famous and radically new definition of poetry in his 1798 *Preface to the Lyrical Ballads*. For Eliot, a literary modernist reacting against Romanticism,

> the only way of expressing emotion in the form of art is by finding an "objective correlative"; in other words, a set of objects, a situation, a chain of events which shall be the formula for that particular emotion, such that when the external facts, which must terminate in a sensory experience, are given, the emotion is immediately evoked.[36]

The problem of *Hamlet*, Eliot thought, was something Shakespeare could not "drag into the light, contemplate, or manipulate into art"—there was no "objective correlative." Although I am proposing here that the various complete and incomplete vessels and the torn, cut, sewn, and plastered objects in our Talmudic story are all also references to R. Eliezer himself, I do not want to allegorize away these objects or the legal discussion. Eliot's attempt to find a better way to describe how objects operate rhetorically in a narrative supports the parallel idea that the author or editor(s) of R. Eliezer's story have subtly made these objects and debates function as literary "objective correlatives" for emotions. Emotions are not only expressed in the story's overt language, but on many indirect levels. Or to use a term from classical rhetoric, the shoe functions as a kind of synecdoche, a part standing for the whole. There is indeed certain poignancy to the sight of an empty shoe after someone has finally departed; the object is so personal and so visibly imprinted with the unique bodily form of its wearer's life. It is a sign of her or his treading various journeys in the world. Thus the pathos of military ceremonies held in memory of soldiers killed in action which display the soldier's helmet poised on his rifle standing over his empty boot.

My main point is that the legal and spiritual meanings converge and merge in the final words R. Eliezer utters. The editors of the Talmud wove the *aggadah* (the nonlegal stories, legends, discussions) and *halakhah* together throughout its pages into one conceptual whole. It would be especially apt to have those two types of discourse coincide on the deepest and most precise level in the story of the passing of a great Sage of the law.

"THE BAN IS ANNULLED! THE BAN IS ANNULLED!"

R. Yehoshua in our story now "stands on his feet" to announce that the ban is annulled, a gesture that parallels and reverses his "standing on his feet" to announce in "The Oven of Akhnai" story that the Torah was "not in heaven," and the law would follow the majority opinion, not R. Eliezer's. But it all seems just a moment too late. Does R. Yehoshua lift the ban *because* of the final dialogue with R. Eliezer or *in spite* of it? Since R. Eliezer has not changed his halakhic stance, why does R. Yehoshua remove the ban at all? Practically speaking, this will prevent his bier from being stoned. Maybe he could not do it while R. Eliezer was alive since he had not recanted. Or maybe there was just not enough time before that moment of expiration. Or it could be that only now that R. Eliezer is gone and no longer a threat or cause of possible factionalization, can he remove the ban. Only now can the Sages recognize and proclaim R. Eliezer's Torah as "pure," since there is no danger of destroying the fabric of the legal system. He can become part of it again. Is this tragically too late, or a final vindication, or both? [37]

The narrator does not tell us. It seems we are meant to infer that R. Eliezer was pure all along, but this was purity not for *this* world, just like that of Elijah the prophet.[38] As great as he was, as intense and unyielding as he was, this world, the world in which the Sages are struggling, the world that they are reconstructing from ruin and trying to infuse with holiness— this world which is decidedly "not heaven," needs special strategies for survival and redemption.[39] But can we afford to be without the purity and zealousness of the Eliezers and Elijahs of this world?

THE FUNERAL OF R. ELIEZER

The story suddenly switches time and place again: it is after the Sabbath. In Jewish law, the body of one who dies on the Sabbath cannot be moved or buried until after the Sabbath concludes.

> At the end of the Sabbath, R. Akiva met his bier being carried from Caesarea to Lydda. [In his grief] he beat his flesh until the blood flowed down upon the ground.

What happens at the death of one's teacher? How does one express and survive the loss? R. Akiva, R. Eliezer's intimate student, takes center stage again at this moment, not Hyrcanus, his son. Akiva dresses in black like a mourner when he informs R. Eliezer of the ban. Here, too, he enacts mourning on behalf of everyone present. His actions and words are a kind of cathartic release of all the emotional tensions built up through the story. The beating of his flesh till blood flows foreshadows and echoes the Talmudic description of R. Akiva's own death, the flaying of his flesh by the Romans in *Berakhot* 61b. The line "till his blood flowed on the ground" moves the focus of the story down towards the ground where R. Eliezer will be buried. But the next line swiftly moves it up towards heaven again:

> R. Akiva began his funeral address as the mourners were lined up about the bier, and said: "'My father, my father, the chariot of Israel and its horsemen!' [2 Kings 2:11–12]. I have many coins, but no money changer to accept them."

R. Akiva quotes the famous anguished line that Elisha, Elijah the Prophet's closest disciple, cries out as he witnesses his teacher suddenly taken up to heaven in a chariot of fire and is separated from him forever:

> As they kept walking and talking, a fiery chariot with fiery horses suddenly appeared and separated one from the other, and Elijah went up to heaven in a whirlwind. Elisha saw it and cried out: "Father! Father! Israel's chariot and its horsemen!" When he could no longer see him, he grasped his garments and rent them in two. (2 Kings 2:11–12)

R. Eliezer and Elijah each pass from this world in traumatic separation from his disciples. But true to form, each passes in a kind of "whirlwind" of purifying fire.

Elijah's relation to Elisha is one of the paradigmatic teacher/student relations in the Bible and Jewish tradition. Like R. Eliezer, Elijah was at first an outsider with an intense zeal for God's pure truth. That pure uncompromising passion made Elijah the great warrior against idol worship but also, ultimately, caused him to fail in his mission as prophet to a people who could not hold to his standard. God relieves him of his mission and directs him to appoint Elisha in his stead in a dramatic passage in the first book of Kings 1:19. Like R. Eliezer in the tale of his beginnings, Elisha is plowing the fields; Elijah appears and wordlessly casts his mantle over him, thereby changing his life and identity in an instant.

Why do teachers of such power fail? R. Askénazi observes that there are two major tendencies in the human personality which lead to the two major causes of failure in educators: (1) the inclination to separation, to excessive spiritual ascent; (2) the inclination to assimilation, to excessive descent to the material and lower realms. Of course, notes R. Askénazi, one whose role is to educate must "descend" to the more base, material world, to the level of the students and raise them up. But therein lies the danger: she herself or he himself will fall and remain on that level, or keep the student on the level of a child. The opposite danger is the very fear of falling; that is, fearing the effects of the descent. The educator will then separate him- or herself and stay too far above.

Both Elijah the Prophet and Eliezer the Sage were among those who sought excessive ascent—purity. Elijah's bodily ascent to heaven without a burial place reflects the very process in his own passing. But these tendencies towards excessive ascent and excessive descent, R. Askénazi notes, also operate inside every person, in every nation, and throughout the entire course of human history.[40] He reads the book of Genesis as humanity's dramatic and painful attempt to find the right balance between these two tendencies, rooted in the proto-typical conflict between Abel and Cain. Abel himself is a failed educator; he does not succeed in guiding his brother Cain towards fraternity and ethics, and so is murdered by Cain. Cain needs to learn to make a place for the other in the world. He is a worker of earth, a firstborn, a man of the material; his name means "acquired, finished." Abel is the brother, the second one, the shepherd, the person of the spirit; his name means "vanishing breath" and his role is to educate Cain in brotherhood. Their very names embody the two conflicting tendencies of excessive desire for ascent and excessive desire for descent.

R. Askénazi perceptively adds that we are also in much need of those who are extreme in their paths to holiness:

> In the long spiritual development of humanity, it is necessary to have heroes of virtue, those who scout out the paths for others. They have to engage in an extremism of virtue, and push beyond the practice of the "golden mean." They open new paths for the future. One must follow them, but not imitate them, for if one tries to imitate them one will fail. They are like the special elite units in a war who go ahead of the regular soldiers and pave the way for others.[41]

In other words, they are the requisite counter-weights to surrendering to a world of limitation and imperfection. This might be another meaning of R. Yohanan's use of the image of the scale in *Pirkei Avot* when he describes R. Eliezer's relation to his other students: R. Eliezer "outweighs" them all. There is an immense force in such personalities. We need them; such fiery uncompromising truth has its critical place in the balance of things. Seen this way, Elijah and R. Eliezer fail on one level, but ascend on another. In their passing, when both leave the earthly realm of ambivalence, concession, and human fallibility, their greatness is luminous. They are lifted heavenwards; their words and deeds are woven back into the tradition, and they become eternal teachers of Israel, though difficult teachers.

At his funeral, R. Eliezer finally is honored as a great rabbinic master with a ritual procession, rows of mourners, and a eulogy from his outstanding student, R. Akiva. It's a bit reminiscent of the end of *Hamlet* where, after all the plot intricacies, duels with poisoned swords, dead bodies strewn about the stage, there is a final formal ritual resolution. Shakespeare's Hamlet is borne up "like a soldier high on the stage," his story itself now lifting him into perpetual memory and honor. Fortinbras takes over, restores the throne, and wishes "flights of angels sing" Hamlet to his rest.

The seventeenth-century Shakespearean martial order, though, is not in the end the rabbinic one. The person who will take up the mantle of R. Eliezer, his student R. Akiva, is at a loss: "I have many coins, but no money-changer to accept them." Levinas comments, "The death of the master [is] the end of questions, the end of answers, a knowledge that cannot be used. Supreme despair. Of whom can I now ask questions?"[42] But why use the image of the money changer for such despair? One needs a money changer when one has come from, or is going to, a foreign country. Or when one needs to break down the large denominations of a foreign currency into the smaller ones necessary for everyday transactions. R. Akiva is now in a foreign country without his teacher, disoriented. He has much knowledge, many traditions, but no one to help him break them down, sort them out, use them for life. How can one use all that currency in this new strange landscape? That is the painful question with which any student grapples after the passing of a great teacher. But he, like every student, has to try to rise out of this darkness. R. Akiva becomes known as one of the great organizers of Jewish traditions. He reconstructs the Torah for the next generation.[43] Teaching and learning go on.

CONTINUING TO LEARN AND TEACH

So the Talmud does not conclude this story with death as an aesthetic climax, as would be the case in a Greek tragedy, or with final words such as Hamlet's "the rest is silence." Here, the rest is not silence, but verbose ongoing debate, more learning and teaching. In the final lines, the story returns Eliezer to his teaching role with its contentious give and take:

> So from this story we see that he learned this law [about penalties for sorcery] from R. Eliezer.—He learned it from R. Eliezer, but did not grasp it, and then he learned it from R. Yehoshua, who made it clear to him.
> But how could R. Eliezer perform such an act of sorcery? Didn't we learn, "if he actually performed magic, he is liable"? The answer is that if it is done only to teach, it is permitted, for it has been said, "You

shall not learn to do after the abominations of these nations [Deut.
18:9]." This means: you are not permitted to learn in order to perform
it, but you are permitted to learn in order to understand and teach.

This question had framed the entire story when it began long ago: from
which teacher did R. Akiva learn the laws about sorcery: R. Eliezer or R.
Yehoshua? At the beginning of the story, the first tradition cited holds that
R. Akiva taught it in the name of R. Yehoshua. But in our long journey
through the story, we find R. Akiva and R. Eliezer together in fields of magic
cucumbers and R. Eliezer testifying that only R. Akiva had asked him about
these laws of sorcery. But teachers like R. Eliezer are not easy to learn from
in all their intensity and in their ascent. It seems that R. Yehoshua, propo-
nent of the view that the Torah "is not in heaven," could make it clearer to
R. Akiva, and so the teaching was ascribed to him. R. Akiva, though, was
himself on a very high level and so intimate with R. Eliezer. Why couldn't
he grasp the teaching? Levinas observes, "Not understood, R. Eliezer's lesson had not been a true teaching. No doubt, R. Akiva had not had the time
to ask all his questions."[44]

Nevertheless, R. Eliezer and R. Yehoshua are doubly reconciled at the
end: (1) R. Yehoshua lifts the ban, and (2) the narrative answers its initial
question by maintaining that *both* of them taught the law about sorcery to
R. Akiva—but in different ways and on different levels. One does not have
to choose between R. Eliezer and R. Yehoshua; they complemented each
other. It is not "either/or" but "both/and."

Yet it also seems that behind the narrative lies another problem about
true teaching and illusory teaching, about forms of sorcery in teaching and
learning, about the ways in which people are bewitched by teachers, and
teachers bewitch others and themselves. Teaching is a dangerous business.
Plato, long ago in his *Gorgias* and *Phaedrus*, inveighed against the first professional teachers—the Sophist rhetoricians of the fifth century BCE—who
taught the arts of persuasion—calling them sorcerers, unconcerned with
true knowledge. How do healthy actions and ideas degenerate into sorcery,
or the deceptive manipulation of others? Sorcery is also a kind of wronging
and injury, a betrayal and manipulation. Was there also a kind of "sorcery"
practiced on R. Eliezer by the Sages when the argument over the oven of
Akhnai culminated in their banning and abandoning him until the day of
his death? In telling these stories, in the ways they are so intricately constructed to raise all these questions, the Sages have also engaged in a brave

self-critique of their own learned culture—even as they lovingly passed it on. Zealousness for the Torah resulted in *ona'at devarim* (verbal wronging) and tragedy. Where, we might ask ourselves, do our own arguments over interpretation and knowledge subtly cross the line into verbal wronging and even "sorcery"? Where do our own academic theories become forms of magic and manipulation? Especially when we take them to be all-explanatory powers?[45]

The tensions in the stories of R. Eliezer are many, and we are continuously on the edge of them—or on the balance pole of a scale—as readers, as teachers, as students, and as human beings. The emblem for these tensions are the walls of the study house in the great debate over the oven of Akhnai, which "still stand," precariously balanced, trying to honor both R. Yehoshua and R. Eliezer: "So they did not fall, in honor of R. Yehoshua, nor did they straighten up, in honor of R. Eliezer. And so they are still standing—leaning" (*Bava Metzi'a* 58a-59b). That there are great and unavoidable costs to these tensions is something else these stories teach us: tensions between tradition and innovation, the legal and the personal, the majority and the minority, parents and children, teachers and students, heavenly truth and earthly truth, sorcery and disillusion, the "pure" and the "impure," faithfulness and abandonment. Wounds, perhaps, are inevitable in all teaching and learning. The story holds all these tensions; the walls are "still standing—leaning"; the house of study, the *beit midrash* contains them as we keep learning and teaching, trying to understand.

R. Yitzhak Luria, known as "Ha-Ari," a sixteenth-century luminary of Jewish mysticism, taught that in the Messianic Era, when the world is fully redeemed and perfected, the law will be decided according to the traditions of R. Eliezer and Beit Shammai, i.e., according to a more strict view. Theirs was a Torah of the higher worlds, different from the Torah of this unredeemed world; in heaven they already decide the law according to R. Eliezer, and so it will be in the future when our world is perfected.[46] In "The Oven of Akhnai" debate, "A heavenly voice then cried out: 'Why do you dispute with R. Eliezer seeing that the *halakhah* agrees with him in every place!'"(*Bava Metzi'a* 58a-59b). Heaven may agree with him "in every place"—but not earth (not yet), where many rabbinic laws are not now decided according to his views.

R. Eliezer has struggled for his words and his truth to be heard from the story of his beginnings, through "The Oven of Akhnai," and now even in his passing. On one level, this story is about isolation, distance, and loss. But there is a counter-narrative of intense connection, intimacy, and life . . . a double movement of the Jewish sensibility itself. It is a narrative of failure and hope intertwined. An acknowledgement of the descents of history, of life moving ineluctably towards the grave, along with a counter-history of ongoing generations—of students and children and teachers who redeem and renew life. Of being "prisoners of hope" regardless of catastrophe, in the famous phrase of the prophet Zechariah (9:12).

We may have to wait to fully grasp R. Eliezer's kind of truth and appreciate his personality, but through these stories he still teaches us all. The Talmud relates that after R. Eliezer died, four Sages entered and tried to argue with one of his teachings. Said R. Yehoshua, "There is no refuting the lion after he is dead" (*Gittin* 83a).

EPILOGUE

R. Yehudah bar Nahman in the name of R. Shimon ben Lakish said:
"When Moses wrote the Torah, a drop of ink was left over in the quill.
He waved it over his head, and it became the rays of glory, as it is said:
'And Moses did not know his face shone' [Exod. 34:29]."

—*Exodus Rabbah* 47:6

RABBI Joseph B. Soloveitchik relates this midrash about the "drop of ink" left over after Moses finished writing the Torah, to the story of R. Eliezer ben Hyrcanus' passing:

> Every great person, however much is written in his books, and how-
> ever much he lectures and discourses publicly—the majority of his
> teachings [*torotav*] remain with him. It is not in his power to pass
> them on to others. As in the words of R. Eliezer, who said to his stu-
> dents in *Sanhedrin* 68a: "Much Torah have I taught and my students
> only took from me as much as a paintbrush from the tube." This is
> what the midrash is referring to when it speaks about the drop of ink
> that was left over in Moses' quill.[1]

Teachers have unfulfilled aches, not only when they conclude their daily lectures, their semesters, their careers, but especially when they must finally depart from the world and their students. In another late essay, R. Soloveitchik, whom I have often cited in this book, wrote eloquently about the meaning of teaching and bravely confessed his own failures as a teacher. He was a Talmudic and intellectual genius and founder of Modern

Orthodoxy in post-World War II America. He was also an awe-inspiring teacher to thousands of disciples who saw him as a major life influence. Yet he was not satisfied. He painfully expressed the absence of the kind of Jewish learning he had absorbed growing up in his illustrious family and traditional community in Europe. His very personal words seem to me a fitting way to conclude this book and so I take the liberty of citing them at some length. His own students in America, he wrote,

> had succeeded in discovering the Torah through scholastic forms of thought, intellectual contact and cold logic . . . but [they have not merited to discover her] through a living, heart-pounding invigorating sense of perception. They know the Torah as an idea, but do not directly encounter her as a "reality" perceptible to taste, sight, and touch.

He had been able, he said, to transmit the cognitive aspect of Torah, the intellectual, expansive, critical side of study. But he had not succeeded in transmitting the other aspect of Torah study, which he describes as an "existential consciousness," one in which the student's "personal existence is filled with living, seething meaning; it takes on new direction and perspective." That aspect of study is part of a

> movement towards the Infinite, and a religious experience: [it is] expressed in complex emotional states of desiring to unite with God and being in awe of that Other . . . where knowledge becomes a fiery faith. The person who, at the depth of his intellectual engagement with the thousands of laws and black letters is 'swept away to God.'"[2]

Religious study, he adds, continually oscillates between the cognitive and non-cognitive: between forcefully asserting intellect and then retracting it when one is overwhelmed by passion, awe, and love; between the mature adult's sophistication and the child's curiosity, enthusiasm, and playfulness.[3] The teacher/student relation, he continues, is modeled upon and enacts this oscillation. On one level, it is a meeting of two knowledgeable and aware adults, who discuss Torah in an intellectual, technical, formal way—a dialogical meeting of minds through language. But on another plane, the teacher and student are like two children at play, enveloped by light and warmth, carried along by the flow of their innocent experience without the need for adult speech and talk. Their communication is not based on the syntactically correct and logical give and take, but on the shared rhythm of pulsating hearts. There is no concerted effort between them, and no outwardly oriented activity that binds them together . . . . Tradition is experiential; its tools are beyond the boundaries of thought and language.[4]

I turn, finally, to two short rabbinic stories which I think well illustrate the dynamic he describes; they are about two other great teachers of Israel separating from their disciples. The first is the Talmud's account of R. Eliezer's disciple, R. Akiva, and his imprisonment by the Romans and condemnation to death for publicly teaching Torah. He is visited by his own great student, R. Shimon bar Yohai (*Pesahim* 112a-b). In that tense and perilous moment, R. Shimon urges, "Teach me Torah!" He does not specify a subject. What does he want—some final life summation, or any word just to know his teacher is not broken? Faced with the loss of his own teacher, he may be imploring, "Just let us continue our relationship—I need you to teach me, to know you are still my teacher." He may be seeking that elusive intimacy R. Soloveitchik was trying to describe, to recapture for a moment that "shared rhythm of pulsating hearts" that is so beyond the cognitive level, to recapture that light and warmth. Perhaps that is one of the meanings of the famous statement R. Yohanan makes in the name of R. Shimon bar Yohai in *Berakhot* 7b:

> A disciple's attending upon a Teacher [shimmushah shel torah] is more valuable than the Teacher's direct teaching. For Scripture says, "Here is Elisha the son of Shafat, who poured water on the hands of Elijah" [2 Kings 3:11]. The text does not say "who studied," but "who poured water." This implies that a disciple's attending upon a Teacher is more valuable than the Teacher's direct teaching.

Or he may also be asking, "What is the Torah for this situation? How do we cope when you and the other great leaders and teachers of Israel are being killed and our people crushed by the Romans?" R. Akiva answers: "I will not teach you." Though he has risked his life before to keep teaching, here he restrains himself. Some commentators explain his refusal as protection of R. Shimon: He could take upon himself the responsibility to risk his own life, but he does not ask it of his student. Maybe, like his own teacher R. Eliezer at the end of his life, R. Akiva also feels the frustrating impossibility of teaching, of not being able to give over all he knows.

"I will not teach you" might also mean that this is not a time for the cognitive, intellectual side of study. Some other kind of teaching is needed. As the dialogue continues between R. Akiva and R. Shimon, R. Akiva says: "More than the calf wants to suck, the cow wants to suckle." Responds R. Shimon, "Yet who is in danger; surely the calf is in danger!" R. Akiva answers, "If you wish to be strangled, be hanged on a large tree, and when you teach your son, teach him from a corrected scroll." There is a word play here on "*lehanik*" (to suckle) and "*lehihanek*" (to get choked or choke yourself). With this double entendre, R. Akiva seems to intimate that learning from him is a life and death matter. It can get you hanged instead of nursed . . . or like a nursling, get choked. I also sense an undertone of ironic jest in this exchange; the double entendre itself reflecting the kind of play R. Soloveitchik describes as part of the intimacy between teacher and student. "Hang yourself from a large tree" can also mean, as commentators suggest, "If you want to assume the life and death responsibility of deciding Jewish law for others, learn it from a great Sage, a tall tree, and cite it in his name." "Hang yourself," i.e., hang your interpretations on those of a great Sage for support and be attached to the tree of tradition so your interpretations will be accepted. He may be hinting—speaking in code in this perilous prison cell under guard—at how to continue the tradition when it is being violently broken by the Romans, when the leaders and heads of Israel are being martyred. The first thing to do is to link yourself to a Sage: "Make yourself a teacher." That is where it all begins, and how it will always continue.

● ● ●

The last story is about Moses' passing and how difficult it was for him to accept that his time to depart had come, that his role as Teacher of Israel was ending. His passing is briefly described in the last chapter of the book of Deuteronomy, which itself concludes the Pentateuch. Traditional midrashic commentary, as usual, fills in many gaps and speculates about what Moses then thought and felt. In the midrashic version of the narrative, Moses asks God for the chance not to die. God replies:

> "This is how I have decided, and this is the way of the world: each generation has its interpreters, its economic guides, its political leaders.

Up to now, you have had your share of service before Me. Now, your time is over and it is your student Yehoshua's turn to serve."

Moses answered: "Master of the world, if I am dying because of Yehoshua, I shall go and be his student!"

God replied: "If this is what you wish, proceed and do it."

Moses rose early and went to Yehoshua's door.

Yehoshua was sitting and interpreting the Divine Word. Moses stood, bent down, and put his hand on his mouth, and Yehoshua did not see him.

The children of Israel appeared at Moses' door to learn Torah from him. They asked, "Where is Moses our Teacher?"

"He has risen early and gone to Yehoshua's door," they were told.

They went and found him at Yehoshua's door. Yehoshua was sitting and Moses standing. They said to Yehoshua, "How can it be that you are sitting and Moses standing?"

Yehoshua lifted his eyes and then saw Moses. He rent his garments, wept and cried: "Teacher! Teacher! Father! Father! Teacher!"

The children of Israel said to Moses," Moses our Teacher, teach us Torah!"

Moses said to them: "I do not have permission."

They said to him: "Do not leave us!"

A voice then came from heaven and said: "Learn from Yehoshua. Accept upon yourselves to sit down and learn from Yehoshua!"

Yehoshua sat in the head position, Moses sat at his right and the sons of Aaron on his left. Yehoshua expounded the Torah in front of Moses.

Rav Shemuel bar Nahman said in the name of R. Yonatan: "When Yehoshua came to the words, 'Blessed is He who chooses among the righteous,' the methodological and pedagogical rules of knowledge were taken away from Moses and given to Yehoshua. Moses no longer understood what Yehoshua was expounding."

After the lesson, the children of Israel asked Moses: "Give to us the concluding words of the Torah!" He replied: "I do not know what to answer," stumbled, and fell.

At that moment, Moses said to God: "Until now I asked for my life, but now my soul is given to you."[5]

In order to hold on, Moses was willing to abandon his role as teacher and become his student's student. But perhaps that is the way of any great teacher, both the way a teacher begins to learn how to be a teacher and the way a teacher ends her career as a teacher. A good teacher *is always* the student of her students. Trying to understand them, worrying about them, learning from them.[6] And knowing when to let go.

This story is a counterpoint to the one with which I began this book, the account of R. Eliezer ben Hyrcanus' becoming a student of R. Yohanan ben Zakkai and a great teacher in his own right, a "Moses" of the Oral Torah. In that story, R. Yohanan had to open the mute "mouth" of R. Eliezer. In this story, Moses undergoes a reverse process, accepting that it is time for him to "close" his mouth. Much is always left unfinished, untransmitted—as R. Eliezer himself so poignantly lamented upon his passing. But those gaps, those blanks, are also the spaces for students to enter, for us to read, renew, recreate, and make these stories and teachings our own.

In another dramatic moment of a great biblical teacher's departure from this world, Elisha asks of his master, Elijah the prophet: "Let a double portion of your spirit pass on to me" (2 Kings 2:9). Elijah answers, "You have asked a hard thing. But if you will see me, as I am taken from you, this will be granted to you; if not, it will not" (2 Kings 2:10). Elisha seems to be asking Elijah to somehow be present with him, as if to say, "I need more of you, your spirit, to be able to cope." Elijah's answer: "The moment you see, I leave and therefore I will be here." Elisha sees what he can't see.[7]

But so it is with any separation of deeply connected people. We see them and do not see them. And we see them differently when they are gone. We are aware more of who they are then; they are "there" and "not there" in a different way now. R. Aaron Kahn, in the eulogy written after the passing of his own great teacher, R. Joseph B. Soloveitchik, quotes Elisha's cry and notes that in the rest of the biblical scene,

> Elijah does not die . . . He was taken into heaven. And the great teachers do not die . . . they are present to us . . . The great holy righteous ones, the *tzaddikim*, in their death are called living . . . They become a living well for their students generation after generation.[8]

Like Elijah, the teacher lives on in two worlds. Or as the Talmud puts it in *Sotah* 13b in a discussion of Moses' passing and the final words of the book of Deuteronomy:

"So Moses died there, the servant of God" [Deut: 34:5] the Great Scribe of Israel. But others declare that Moses never died. It is written here, "So Moses died *there*" [Deut. 34:5], and elsewhere it is written: "And he was *there* with God" [Exod. 34:28]. Just as in the latter passage it [the word "there"] means "standing and ministering," so also here [it means he is still] "standing and ministering."

But still, there is a time for parting and for a student to go on by her- or himself, to become a teacher and give to others, to move from the level of "daughter," to "sister," to "mother," to use the metaphors of R. Eliyahu, the Talmudic genius of the eighteenth century known as the "Ga'on of Vilna." To go from being a passive absorber, to a colleague, to an independent, generative teacher who raises up many other students.

I conclude this book also feeling the ache of having much more left to say but needing finally to pass this work on to my readers. May this book also be generative and help give birth to students and colleagues and teachers who bring goodness, wisdom, life, and love to the world.

NOTES

Preface

Epigraph: From Franz Rosenzweig, "The Builders," in *On Jewish Learning*, ed. N. N. Glatzer (NY: Schocken, 1965), 76.

1   The lectures were filmed and are available online at: http://www.uwtv.org/video/series.aspx?&id=1549962905.

2   Maimonides, Commentary on *Pirkei Avot*. The verb "imagine" here is somewhat perplexing. For Maimonides, in his *Guide for the Perplexed*, imagination is a lower faculty, albeit one needed for prophecy. "Imagine" is the English translation of the verb used in Ibn Tibbon's medieval Hebrew translation of Maimonides's original Arabic: *tedammeh*. In the version of Maimonides's commentary on *Pirkei Avot* edited by the modern Maimonides scholar, Rav Kapah, which contains both the Arabic and the Hebrew, one finds that the original Arabic phrase Maimonides uses is *"takil lahu ta'alim"* (You should measure out to him [or: allot to him] instruction). Rav Kapah understands the passage to mean, "You should consider him to be your teacher so that you will have a give-and-take with him," exchange opinions, tell him what you know, and hear his response (411). Rav Kapah thinks Ibn Tibbon mistakenly read the Arabic word *takil* as *takhil* and mistranslated it as "imagination." In any case, Maimonides seems to mean that even if your teacher is someone lower than you in wisdom, by learning together in a give-and-take your knowledge will be strengthened. I thank Charles Mannekin for helping clarify this linguistic point in an e-mail to me on October 25, 2006, which I have paraphrased in this note.

3   Jane Tomkins, "Pedagogy of the Distressed," *College English* 10 (1990): 656. See also her *A Life in School: What the Teacher Learned* (Boston: Addison-Wesley, 1996).

4   Dekunle Samade, undergraduate senior at the University of Maryland, College Park, qtd. in Jeffrey Young, "Actually Going to Class, for a Specific Course? How Twentieth-Century," *Chronicle of Higher Education*, Feb. 27, 2011, http://chronicle.com/article/Actually-Going-to-Class-How/126519/.

Introduction

Epigraphs: Friedrich Nietzsche to Franz Overbeck, 1884, quoted in George Steiner, *Lessons of the Masters* (Cambridge, MA: Harvard University Press, 2003), 116; Franz Rosenzweig, in Nahum Glatzer, *Franz Rosenzweig: His Life and Thought* (NY: Schocken, 1966), 216.

1   See my other essays on pedagogy and student/teacher relations listed in the bibliography.
2   Oral comments in his "Models of Learning in Jewish Mysticism," (paper presented at the Summer School of the Institute for Advanced Study, Hebrew University, Jerusalem, June 26, 1998).
3   Ibid.
4   Rabbi Joseph B. Soloveitchik, *And From There You Shall Seek: U-vikkashtem mi-sham*, trans. Naomi Goldlum (New York: Ktav, 2008), 142.
5   R. Reuven Ziegler, from his series of online essays and archives of the philosophy of Rav Soloveitchik, "Introduction to the Philosophy of Rav Soloveitchik," http://www.vbm-torah.org/archive/ravindex.htm, accessed March 2, 2009. R. Soloveitchik, in a memorial lecture for his wife in 1971, further says:

> Can the Oral Torah pass on kedusha [holiness] . . . in the sense that the written Torah sanctifies tefillin, mezuzah, the Torah Parchment, etc.? It would be folly to conclude that the Oral Torah is inferior in this respect. The answer is that the Oral Torah operates in a more subtle manner, transmitting sanctity through study and its relation to the mind of the student . . . The parchment of talmud Torah is the human mind, the human heart and personality . . . The old halakhic equation that every Jew is a sefer Torah (Torah scroll) is, in this light, fully understandable. The living Jew is the sefer Torah of the *Torah she be-al peh*, the Oral Torah. (Lecture 11, "Torah and Humility," http://www.vbm-torah.org/archive/rav/rav11.htm)

6   "House of Searching" would be a felicitous literal translation of the phrase *Beit Midrash*.
7   The technique of learning in small groups or pairs has been rediscovered in the past several years by secular educational theorists, who have dubbed it "co-operative learning." Its advocates support their work with the postmodern claim that all knowledge is social, dialogic, and communal. They offer abundant evidence of the effectiveness of co-operative learning and its success in creating classroom community, a truth I can affirm from my own use of these techniques in my classes. See especially the work of Aliza Segal, *Hevruta Study: History, Benefits, and Enhancements* (Jerusalem: Academy for Torah Initiatives and Directions, 2003). Historically, it is not clear exactly how students learned in the early rabbinic period, or exactly when the method of studying in pairs

entered the later yeshiva world. See Shaul Stampfer, *Ha-Yeshivah ha-Lita'it be-Hit'havutah* (Jerusalem, Zalman Shazar, 1975).

8   See R. Léon Askénazi, "Temps du mérite et temps du retour," in *La Parole et l'écrit*, ed. Marcel Goldmann, vol. 1 (Paris: Albin Michel, 1999), 356, 385 [All translations mine]. Along with Emmanuel Levinas and Andre Néher, Askénazi was one of the great intellectual luminaries of post-World War II French Jewry. Like them, he dedicated himself to reconnecting French Jews with Jewish tradition, and grappled with the problems of modernity, Zionism, and the Holocaust. Askénazi, though, is almost unknown in the English-speaking world. Translations of his work are just beginning to appear in Hebrew. I hope that my many notes and references to him in this book will begin to introduce his thought to a wider audience.

9   R. Yitzhak Hutner stresses that the Sages intentionally wrote the Oral Torah down in such a way as to keep it "oral"; that is, in such a way that its written form would need the assistance of oral explanation, and the written text would not come to substitute for hearing and receiving Torah from mouth to ear. He further analyzes how the connection of the *Berit* (covenant) with Israel to Oral Torah is a matter of the fundamental connection of God and Israel over and above any specific contents of the Torah. See Hutner, *Pahad Yitzhak*, vol. 1 *Hanukkah, Ma'amar* 1 (Brooklyn: Gur Aryeh Institute, 1995), 27–29.

10 R. Léon Askénazi, "Unité et pluralité dans la loi orale," in *La Parole et l'écrit*, ed. Marcel Goldmann, vol. 2 (Paris: Albin Michel, 2005), 329–30. R. Askénazi appears to be basing some of his ideas here and above on R. Yitzhak Hutner's *Pahad Yitzhak*, which was a strong influence on him. Though Askénazi does not refer to it, the first essay in the volume, *Hanukkah*, of the *Pahad Yitzhak* cited in the previous note discusses this deeper relation of Written and Oral Torah, and the Talmudic discussion in tractate *Gittin* 60.

11 See the use of this midrash in the classic work of R. Hayyim of Volozhin, (1749–1821) in *Nefesh ha-Hayyim*, part 1, ch. 16. The way I am summarizing the ideas in this reference to R. Hayyim Volozhin is itself a piece of "Oral Torah,"; it comes from notes made in a study session with one of my own teachers in Jerusalem, Rav Marc Kujavski, dealing with "The Land of Israel and its Kedushah," October 17, 2007.

12 Hannah Arendt, "The Crisis in Education," *Between Past and Future: Eight Exercises in Political Thought* (New York: Penguin, 1961), 192, 196. See also Hannah Arendt, *The Jewish Writings* (New York: Schocken, 2007).

13 R. Hutner discusses the digressive nature of the Oral Torah and its difference from more classical Western forms of intellectual discourse in various essays in his *Pahad Yitzhak*. In *Ma'amar* 8, he analyzes a Talmudic passage in *Shabbat* 138b-139a, which discusses the period after the destruction of the Second Temple, the Hadrianic persecutions and exiles, their connection to the digressive nature of the Oral Torah and its seeming lack of logical, linear lucidity. R. Hutner cites R. Yehudah Loew ben Bezalel (1524–1609), known as "Maharal of Prague," in his comments on this Talmudic passage. I paraphrase as follows:

Because Israel and the Torah are one, the structure of Torah is like the dispersed Jewish people: it, too, is scattered and dispersed. Israel are one people scattered amongst the nations; so too is the very form of Torah. One needs to "wander" back and forth inside the Torah itself. The answers, the meanings are not found in any one place. This makes the Torah an object of scorn for those whose forms of wisdom are clear, well-ordered, and structured. I find this interpretation an interesting theological understanding of Talmudic rhetoric and hermeneutics.

14   Emmanuel Levinas, "Desacralization and Disenchantment," in *Nine Talmudic Readings*. ed. and trans. Annette Aronowicz (Bloomington, IN: Indiana University Press, 1994), 142.

15   R. Shlomo Carlebach, as recorded and edited by Shmuel Zevin, *Lev ha-Shamayim: Sihot ve-Sippurim al Pesah*, 2nd ed. (Jerusalem: n.p., 2008), 223. [Translation mine].

16   John Keats, letter to his brother on 21 December 1817 in John Keats and H. Buxton Forman, *The Letters of John Keats* (London: Kessling, 2004), 57.

17   For an excellent survey in English and application of the academic historicist approach to rabbinic stories, combined with more recent literary approaches, see Jeffrey L. Rubenstein's books, *Talmudic Stories: Narrative Art, Composition and Culture* (Baltimore: Johns Hopkins University Press, 2003) and *Stories of the Babylonian Talmud* (Baltimore: Johns Hopkins University Press, 2010).

18   Walter Benjamin, "The Task of the Translator," in *Illuminations*, ed. Hannah Arendt (New York: Schocken, 1969), 71.

19   Despite an exhaustive bibliographical search, I have found no direct source in the writings of Tillich for this quotation. It may well be an oral teaching of his—a teaching he would often say to his students, which was then repeated by them in his name, but never written down.

20   R. Nahman of Bratslav, "*Patah Rabbi Shimon*," #60: paragraphs 5–7, in *Likkutei Moharan* (1808; Jerusalem: Agudat Meshek ha-Nahal, 1959). Maria Harris, in her *Teaching and the Religious Imagination* (New York: HarperCollins, 1987), has also described teaching via indirection using Kierkegaard's Christian existentialist idea of "indirect communication." See R. Adin Steinsaltz, *Opening the Tanya* (San Francisco: Josey-Bass, 2003), 60, 98, for a lucid explanation in English for those without background in these traditions. In literary theory, the modern field of "narratology" has flourished in an attempt to formalistically account for how stories function and affect their readers. See, for example, the works of Gérard Genette, Tzetvan Todorov, Roland Barthes, Wayne Booth, Mieke Bal, Gerald Prince, Paul Ricœur, Susan Lanser, Lisa Zunshine and others.

21   I am sympathetic here to R. Léon Askénazi's emphasis on a "return to Hebrew" as a key part of the philosophical method he learned from Jacob Gordin (1896–1947), a brilliant Russian-Jewish refugee philosopher and Jewish studies scholar. This meant, as Askénazi defines it, the "rehabilitation of the immediate intuitions of Jewish consciousness as a coherence of thought." He also took the idea of history as engenderment (or *toledot* in Hebrew) from Gordon, who called it "historiosophy," the meaning of history according to the Hebrew prophets.

History is not the fatalistic world of the Greeks, nor a succession of anonymous events, but an ongoing engenderment of human identities; it is the dramatic scene of ethical and spiritual struggle as the generations are birthed, struggle, and move towards an ultimate redemption. "Jacob Gordin, mon maître" in *Jacob Gordin, Écrits: le renouveau de la pensée juive en France*, ed. Marcel Goldmann (Paris: Albin Michel, 1995), 14–16. See my essay on Askénazi, "The Philosopher, the Rabbi, and the Rhetorician," *College English* 72, no. 6 (2010): 590–607.

22   Nevertheless, in recent years, many academic literary theorists have become interested in pedagogy, instead of devaluing it as a minor, less rigorous field to be relegated to the "Education Department." For postmodern thought has emphasized the need to examine what is marginalized, to question theoretical structures, to be humble about the possibilities of absolute or objective knowledge, and to attend to the power relations implicit in every act of knowing. I would add that the daily classroom, in all its surprise, uncertainty, and disruption is certainly a place where those tendencies are lived out (usually unplanned), as any exhausted teacher can vouch at the end of the day.

23   The nature of "performance" and "performance theory" is the subject of much current theoretical concern in literary study, and postmodern thought. A few of the key theorists in this area are J. L. Austin, Judith Butler, Richard Schechner. Shakespeare studies in particular have developed "performance theory" both as a means of understanding Shakespeare's texts and as a pedagogy for teaching them. See for example, *Teaching Shakespeare Through Performance*, ed. Milla Cozart Riggio (New York: Modern Language Association of America, 1999).

24   Rosenzweig, "The New Thinking," in Glatzer, *Franz Rosenzweig*, 204–5.

25   R. Joseph B. Soloveitchik, *Nefesh ha-Rav*, ed. Hershel Shachter (Jerusalem: Reshit Yerushalayim, 1994), 290–91.

26   R. Nahman of Bratslav, *Sefer ha-Middot*, (1821; Warsaw: n.p., 1912), 112–13 (also qtd. in Louis I. Newman, *Hasidic Anthology* (New York: Schocken, 1963), 25.

Chapter 1

Epigraph: From R. Léon Askénazi, "Morale et sainteté: Étude des Pirké-Avot—Ch 1 Mishna 1," in *Mayanot: Cours transcrits du Rav Léon Askénazi-Manitou*, no. 5 (Jerusalem: Foundation Manitou, 1993), 10.

1   Burials were not allowed inside Jerusalem due to both its sanctity and the biblical prohibition that priests (*Kohanim*) not come into contact with the dead.

2   My translation of the story here is mostly based on that of Judah Goldin, *The Fathers According to Rabbi Nathan*, recension A, ch. 6 (New York: Schocken, 1955), 41. However, I have made some of my own minor grammatical and stylistic changes to his English rendition that I will not mark in the text. The original texts are unpunctuated, so the paragraph and line spacing are mine as well. When the text is translated from the Hebrew more literally but less elegantly, as I do here, several key literary, thematic, and structural features become clearer.

See also the parallel but different versions of this story in other rabbinic sources, including *Avot de-Rabbi Natan*, recension B, 12–13 and *Pirkei de-Rabbi Eliezer*, ch. 1–2. I have chosen this one since it seems to me the most interesting and sophisticated from a literary point of view.

3   For an extensive excellent discussion and survey of the use of these images in biblical and rabbinic literature, see Michael Fishbane, "The Well of Living Water: A Biblical Motif and Its Ancient Transformations," in *"Sha-arei Talmon': Studies in the Bible, Qumran, and the Ancient Near East Presented to Shemaryahu Talmon*, ed. Michael Fishbane and Emmanuel Tov (Winona Lake, IN: Eisenbrauns, 1992), 3–16.

4   Perhaps only someone such as the famous modern Jewish mystic, Talmudic scholar, and first Chief Rabbi of Palestine, R. Avraham Yitzhak Kook, can well explain this paradoxical relation between never uttering a word one did not hear from one's teacher and the flow of unique prophetic creative insight. I take the liberty to quote him at length:

> Understanding reached by one's own mind—this is the highest expression of spiritual progress. All that is learned by study is absorbed from the outside and is of lesser significance as compared with what is thought through with the soul itself. All that is acquired by study is only a profound strategy as to how to draw on what is hidden in the heart, in the depths of the soul, one's inner understanding, from the knowledge within.
>
> Knowledge in our inner being continues to stream forth. It creates, it acts.
>
> The higher creative individual does not create. He only transfers. He brings a vital, new light from the higher source where originality emanates to the place where it has not previously been manifest, from the place that "no bird of prey knows, nor has the falcon's eye seen it" (Job 28:7), "that no man has passed, nor has any person inhabited it" (Jer. 2:6).
>
> And with the emergence of such a greatness of the self, there is fashioned the faithful ear, the listening heart. Such a person will never utter a word he did not hear from his teacher. These are the prophets of truth and righteousness, to whom God has communicated the truth.

R. Avraham Yitzhak Kook, *Abraham Isaac Kook: The Lights of Penitence, the Moral Principles, Lights of Holiness, Essays, Letters, and Poems*, trans. Ben-Zion Bokser, vol. 1 of *Orot HaKodesh* (N.Y: Paulist Press, 1978), 216–17.

5   Maimonides, the authoritative medieval codifier of Talmudic and Jewish law, devotes an entire section of his "Laws of Torah Study" to the balancing and priorities in the relations between parents and children, teachers and students. See his *Mishneh Torah*, "Laws of Torah Study," especially ch. 1–6.

6   I am grateful to Japhet Johnstone for this idea and its formulation.

7   Walter Benjamin, "Franz Kafka: On the Tenth Anniversary of His Death," in *Illuminations*, ed. Hannah Arendt (New York: Schocken, 1969), 117.

8   Erich Auerbach, *Mimesis: The Representation of Reality in Western Literature*, trans. Willard Trask (Princeton, NJ: Princeton University Press, 1953), 11.

9   Rachel Adelman, *The Return of the Repressed: Pirqe de-Rabbi Eliezer and the Pseudepigrapha* (Leiden: Brill, 2009), 31.

10   R. Léon Askénazi, *Sod ha-Ivri*, 62–64; *Ki Mitsion: La calendrier hebraique* (Jerusalem: Foundation Manitou, 1999), 2:38–40; *Ki MiTsion: Notes sur la Paracha* (Jeursalem: Foundation Manitou, 1997), 1:215–17, 223–25.

I roughly translate and paraphrase some of his further ideas on feeding the body and the spirit as follows. There are two seemingly opposite dimensions to human existence: the "what" *(mah),* one's physical body given over to deterministic natural law; and the "who" *(mi),* one's consciousness and intellect. The physical connection between the world and the person is food, "And in the sweat of your brow, you shall eat bread" (Gen 13:19). Food is the world that is transformed into the human. When a person ceases eating, he or she first loses the "who," and then the "what" through death.

In a commentary on the first chapters of the book of Leviticus, which describes various "sacrifices" brought to the Temple to be used by the priests on the altar to effect expiation for sins, Askénazi further notes that the process of expiation here is essentially one of consummation—either by fire or through a meal eaten by the Temple priests—and composed specifically of foods that nourish humans. Every sin ultimately emanates from our primordial appetite for pleasure, but that appetite at the same time is necessary because it assures the functioning of bodily life and allows for self-consciousness. But human existence, then, inextricably involves an economic and moral problem because each person—by the very fact of living life in this world—must have appetite and eat, and compete for its resources. No wonder, then, that in the biblical narrative, the first sin of the first man (Adam) is inevitably tied to a problem of food.

Jewish law, then, compensates for this existential moral and economic problem through the Temple ritual, which is that of a "meal, in the obtaining of which no fault has been committed." The *kodashim,* the consecrated food offerings, have been removed from the market economy of exchange and surplus value. In this sense, he continues, one could describe the cult of the High Priest of the Temple of Jerusalem as the "perfect man, dressed in perfect garments, in the perfect house, nourished by the perfect meal." In other words, "If we could live or emulate the holiness of the priest exempted from the risks of the economic life, our meal would also be without fault." The ordinary Jew participates by bringing these sacrifices to the Temple priests. These offerings are then slaughtered or burned on the Temple altar, and in certain cases partially eaten by the priests. In R. Askénazi's view, the entire act produces a certain form of consciousness; it creates the possibility for an existence untainted by the existential moral and economic problem, allows for expiation and for renewed good conscience.

When the Temple was destroyed, R. Eliezer and his colleagues had to find new ways to re-create and transfer the lost holiness and rituals of the Jerusalem

Temple to the daily life of the people. This was one of the great projects of rabbinic Judaism and the Oral Torah of the Pharisees, as we'll see further in chapter 2.

11   For a thorough review of all the images of sucking as transmission in rabbinic and kabbalistic sources, see Ellen Haskell, "Metaphor and Symbolic Representation: The Image of God as a Suckling Mother in Thirteenth-Century Kabbalah" (PhD. diss., University of Chicago, 2005).

Ora Wiskind-Elper, in her commentary on the teachings of the Hasidic master R. Ya'akov of Izbica-Radzyn, cites a penetrating comment of his about why the things we learned as children and things that are strikingly original endure in consciousness more than information we accumulate later in life. The Sages call this kind of novelty in learning *girsa de-yankuta* (learning of one's youth). Of this, R. Ya'akov writes: "When a baby [*tinok*; in Aramaic, *yanuka*] nurses from its mother's breasts, it draws forth milk that had never before existed. That milk had naught a moment to 'get old'; its taste is better than anything 'already there.' As it says of the shew-bread [*lehem ha-pannim*], 'Hot bread is placed there' [1 Sam. 21:17]—that bread never staled; it was forever fresh." Ora Wiskind-Elper, *Wisdom of the Heart: The Teachings of Rabbi Ya'akov of Izbica-Radzyn* (Philadelphia: Jewish Publication Society, 2010), 33. She is citing *Beit Ya'akov* 1, *Vayehi* 72.

The baby, that is, draws forth milk meant for her or him alone and created by her or his need; the milk is endlessly "new" yet still intimately attached to its source. Our intense desire to learn as children, the newness of everything, a close attachment to the divine Source, give us great pleasure; when things become habitual, mastered, old, distant from their source, the pleasure is diminished.

12   See the poignant essay by R. Joseph B. Soloveitchik analyzing Moses as the "nursing-father" [*omen*] described in Num 11:11–15 and the significance of this metaphor in "Teaching with Clarity and Empathy," in *Reflections of the Rav: Lessons in Jewish Thought Adapted from the Lectures of Rabbi Joseph B. Soloveitchik*, ed. Abraham R. Besdin (Jerusalem: Dept. of Torah Education, Wizo, 1979). Protests Moses to God, "Was it I who conceived this entire people? Was it I who brought them forth, that You should say to me, "Carry them in your bosom as a nurse carries a nursing infant, to the land which You swore to their fathers'"?

Moses, in R. Soloveitchik's reading, at first resists this role, but then realizes it is not enough to be a leader, but he also has to become an *omen*, a patient, emotionally sympathetic "nursing father" to a temperamental, plaintive childish people undergoing a national infancy. Today as well, R. Soloveitchik adds, teachers need to be in the nursing role as much as the intellectually commanding role, and teaching requires "the warm embrace as much as the brilliant idea, readiness to subordinate career and egotism, like the nursing mother who merges her identity with that of the suckling child, and puts its needs over her own" (158). See also his "Engaging the Heart and Teaching the Mind" in this same volume, on two typologies of king-teacher and saint-teacher (160–68).

R. Yitzhak Hutner, in a transcript of a talk he delivered to young yeshivah students about teaching and learning, quotes a young student who describes his relation to his teacher of secular studies as being like a person who receives food from the hand of the cook; whereas his relation to his "Rebbe," his teacher of Jewish studies, is like one who receives food from his wet nurse. The nurse nourishes the suckling with the essence of her own life; the cook, however, only gives something that has come from the outside, and mechanically processes the food. *Pahad Yitzhak, Iggerot u-Khetavim*, 134–35.

The Talmud, *Berakhot* 10a notes the grace of God in situating women's breasts in a "*mekom binah*" (a place of understanding) near her heart, so that nursing is a personal face-to-face relation of mother and infant, as opposed to placing the breasts on the underside of the body as is the case with animals.

13   A contemporary kabbalistic commentary on *Pirkei Avot* notes that R. Eliezer corresponds to the divine emanation—or *sefirah*—of *Malkhut*. In the kabbalistic schema of the ten divine emanations which structure the world, the attribute of *Malkhut* is the final "vessel" and "container" for all the previous divine influences and "has nothing of its own." It also represents speech and "Kingship"— insofar as the King is the servant of the people and channels sustenance to them all. *Malkhut* also connotes the highest attribute of *Keter* (crown). See R. Rafael Moshe Luria, *Beit Genazai: Perushim le-Massekhet Avot* (Jerusalem, published by the author, 2002), 108–10.

14   Melila Hellner-Eshed in personal conversation. I also thank her for many insights on the topic of Mentor and Disciple in Jewish thought.

15   R. Daniel Landes, director, Pardes Institute of Jewish Studies, Jerusalem, in a personal conversation about this story.

16   Melila Hellner-Eshed, *A River Issues from Eden: The Language of Mystical Experience in the Zohar* (Palo Alto, CA: Stanford University Press, 2009), 136. See also Franz Rosenzweig's commentary on the physical and spiritual languages of eros in the Song of Songs:

> The analogue of love permeates as analogue of all revelation. It is the ever-recurring analogy of the prophets. But it is precisely meant to be more than an analogy . . . it is not enough that God's relation to man is explained by the simile of the lover and the beloved. God's word must contain the relationship of lover to beloved directly, the significant, that is, without pointing to the significate. And so we find it in the Song of Songs . . . the I and Thou of human discourse is without more ado also the I and Thou between God and man. The distinction between immanence and transcendence disappears in language . . . . Man loves because God loves and as God loves.

"Revelation, or the Ever-Renewed Birth of the Soul," in *The Star of Redemption*, trans. William Hallo (Notre Dame, IN: Notre Dame Press, 1970), 199.

17   The Ga'on here notes a parallel interpretation of his on a midrash on the Song of Songs 3:11, where these three stages in the teacher-student relationship are compared to the feminine archetypes of "daughter," "sister," and "mother."

18　See also the continuation of our passage in *Avot de-Rabbi Natan*, ch. 6, about R. Eliezer's beginnings, which goes on to discuss these three men further and what happened in the siege of Jerusalem.

19　E-mail message to the author, December 26, 2009.

20　See Wayne Booth's classic work of literary criticism, *The Rhetoric of Fiction* (Chicago: University of Chicago Press, 1961) for a sophisticated analysis of the many levels of narration in any given story, especially the difference between the "real historical author or editor" and the "implied author" or narrator and various sub-narrators within the tale. There are various levels of narration and reading in the story of R. Eliezer as well.

21　I use the verb "birthing" here to describe this interaction between R. Yohanan and R. Eliezer. But we should distinguish this pedagogical process from the classical Socratic method. In Plato's *Theaetetus*, Socrates uses the famous metaphor of the "midwife" to describe his technique, in which the teacher seeks to elicit from the student what the teacher already knows and considers as latent in the student's mind. The teacher "births" this latent knowledge through opening/questioning the student in dialogue. (The method is called *maieutics*, from the Greek word for "midwifery," which Socrates also claims was his mother's profession). As part of the process, the student can also discover her or his own ignorance, especially if she or he begins with a dogmatic, unexamined presumption of already knowing.

　　To further clarify the difference, I take the liberty of once again quoting R. Askénazi since a central aim of his work was to carefully distinguish between Jewish and Greek philosophical language and modes of thought. The following comments also elaborate on the quotation of his which I have used for the epigraph of this chapter: "In the Talmudic definition, a teacher is not someone who has students, but someone who has had a teacher." I summarize here from his *Sod Midrash ha-Toledot* I, ed. and trans. Hayyim Rotenberg (Jerusalem: Beit El, 2009), 451. A caveat: these comments are a rough outline of a complex passage creatively analyzing biblical, mishnaic, Talmudic, and kabbalistic passages and ideas; they require a far longer and detailed exposition than I have space for here.

　　The Hebrew word used in Talmudic literature to denote a highly learned Sage is *talmid hakham*, which translates literally as "student of the wise." The difference between a *talmid hakham* and the general non-Jewish model of a philosopher or Sage, Askénazi contends, is that the greatness of the non-Jewish teacher is usually measured by the number of students he or she has. In Israel, by contrast, a person is measured according to the greatness of the teacher or Rabbi with whom he or she studied and to whom he or she is closely attached, both intellectually and personally. Hence the Sages of Israel are called "*students of the wise*" (*talmidei hakhamim*).

　　In Jewish tradition, the student serves as the teacher's midwife, rather than the reverse. How so? To begin with, wisdom and truth are not seen as possessed by, or belonging to, the teacher, but only transferred through him or her as a conduit. If the student just uses the "philosophical method" to gain knowledge, asks and answers questions to her or himself, she or he will remain in doubt. When Rabban Gamaliel, in a famous passage in the Mishnah in *Pirkei Avot* 1:16 says, "Find yourself a teacher, and remove yourself from doubt," he is referring to such a situation. Why do I need a teacher in this case? Not to receive knowledge, but to remove the doubt that the philosophical mode of thinking has engendered.

But that, Askénazi observes, is not yet wisdom in the Jewish sense. Knowledge and wisdom come from a deeper dimension and different dynamic in the teacher/student relationship, one alluded to later in *Pirkei Avot* 6:3–4. This passage prescribes that someone who "learns even one letter" from a friend "has to call him his teacher." Asks Askénazi, but what does this mean? What is the importance of "one letter"? A "letter," he answers, citing a complex source elsewhere in the Talmud, "is the name of God" (*Berakhot* 33a). So, "one who conveys to another person the meaning of the letter as the name of God is in the category of his teacher." To clarify Askénazi's point a bit further, I should add that in kabbalistic tradition, the Hebrew letters and names of God and their permutations, signify deeper revelations of Divinity, and the ways in which the Infinite connects to the finite. The entire Torah is thus interpreted in a non-linear, non-narrative sense to be the "Names of God." So, continues Askénazi, in the Jewish tradition the student asks, and the teacher answers. Only on this deeper level of understanding the meaning of the letters is it possible to remove oneself from doubt. And in this sense, the student "gives birth to the teacher," calls her or him "teacher," and as the famous Talmudic saying has it, "Much have I learned from my teachers, more from my colleagues, but from my students most of all" (*Ta'anit* 7a).

I must add, however, that there are many models of students and teachers in Jewish sources, and Askénazi is broadly generalizing here to make a certain larger polemical point. But I think his insight helps illuminate the conclusion of our story of R. Eliezer and R. Yohanan when R. Yohanan says "Rabbi Eliezer, Master, you have taught me the truth!" We'll see more of R. Eliezer's proficiencies in the deeper mysteries of the Torah in chapter 3.

Chapter 2

1   For an excellent analysis of this story and an exhaustive bibliography of the many interpretations written about it, see Jeffrey L. Rubenstein's account in "Torah, Shame, and the 'Oven of Akhnai'" in his *Talmudic Stories: Narrative Art, Composition, and Culture* (Baltimore: Johns Hopkins University Press, 1999), 34–63.

2   See my *Slayers of Moses: The Emergence of Rabbinic Interpretation in Modern Literary Theory* (Albany: SUNY Press, 1982), 40 ff.

3   There is a different version of the story in the Jerusalem Talmud, *Mo'ed Katan* 3:1. It has all the same plot elements but in a different and less dramatic arrange-

ment. I have made some minor adjustments to the translation found in the Soncino English edition of the Talmud. I have also cut some of the preliminary context of the narrative in the interests of space. The abrupt leaps, unclear pronouns and sudden juxtapositions are characteristic of Talmudic style, and part of its conscious rhetorical construction. The Talmud's editors also assume an audience with the background to follow the legal discussion.

The name "Rabban" for Rabban Gamaliel is used for those Rabbis who in ancient times were Presidents or Heads of the Sanhedrin, the Jewish High Court. I have left it as is in the text instead of abbreviating it to" R." for "Rabbi" since "Rabban" indicates a higher level of authority.

4   See, for example, the extensive commentary on this aspect of the story by Menachem Fisch in his *Rational Rabbis: Science and Talmudic Culture* (Bloomington, IN: Indiana University Press, 1997), 51–92.

5   Among attempts to connect the specific technical legal issue with the larger drama and meaning of the story, especially interesting is that of the rabbinic commentator known as "Malbim," an acronym for R. Meir Leibush ben Yechiel Michel (1809–1879), discussed in note 11 below, and the lengthy analysis by a commentator known as "Radal," the acronym for R. David Luria (1798–1855), in the introduction to his edition of *Pirkei de-Rabbi Eliezer* (Warsaw, 1852).

6   A particularly interesting analysis of aggadic portions of rabbinic literature from a theological point of view is found in the works of the commentator known as "Maharal" of Prague, R. Yehudah Loew, (1520–1609), especially his *Be'er ha-Golah* and *Hiddushei Aggadot*. (He is more popularly known as the famous creator of the "Golem.") Innovative contemporary literary, psychological, and theological readings of midrashic texts are offered by Aviva Zornberg in her various recent books.

7   The final division of the Mishnah tractate *Tohorot* deals with the rules of ritual purity and impurity. Its first and largest tractate, *Kelim* (vessels), examines different levels of purity and impurity, how they affect various substances and in what ways they are transmitted. The strongest level of *tumah* is called *avi avot ha-tumah* which means the "father of fathers of *tumah*." It occurs through direct contact with a corpse. The next, more common, level is called *av ha-tumah* (father of *tumah*). That includes one who touched a human corpse, the carcass of one of the eight species of *sheretz* (creeping things which are not in the category of kosher food), the carcass of an animal that died by means other than ritual slaughtering, and various other categories. Vessels and foods can acquire *tumah* as well. An oven might acquire *tumah* depending on what kinds of objects reach its inner space, or what and whom it comes in contact with.

8   R. Marc Kujavski alerted me to this association of completeness and incompleteness to *tumah* and *taharah* in rabbinic law and its possible deeper meanings in a seminar in Jerusalem in October, 2008. I summarize my understanding of his ideas and the way he connected them to "The Oven of Akhnai" story as follows: If something is completed and finished by human action, then it is susceptible to *tumah*. If something is unfinished by human action, incomplete, it is NOT

susceptible to *tumah*. In this light, when the Sages opposing R. Eliezer say of the Torah, "It is not in heaven" in our story, they would be saying that it comes under human control and so can reach a state of "completion"; therefore, they see the oven of Akhnai as a complete vessel and so able to receive *tumah*. But for R. Eliezer, Torah is still connected to heaven, and is not completed; he views the oven as incomplete and thus *tahor* (pure). R. Kujavski suspects that if one looked at all the halakhic debates in the Talmud between R. Eliezer and the Sages one would see this same principle run through all.

I would further stress that the oven in his reading is not simply functioning as a metaphor for Torah; rather the same conceptual principle would underlie both the legal case and the metaphysical debate about the status of Torah, which extends far beyond this one story. Moreover, this reading would make R. Eliezer not the rigid conservative clinging to a closed tradition, but someone still connected to a "prophetic" openness of Torah: in other words, Torah is "incomplete," still open and connected to a heavenly prophetic source, not under human control. Thus all the miracles and supernatural proofs to which R. Eliezer resorts. For more discussion of the relation of completeness, infinity, and purity, and R. Kujavski's connection of the Akhnai story to kabbalistic speculations, see note 21 below.

9   See Mishnah *Kelim* 5:10 and *Eduyyot* 7:7; Tosefta *Eduyyot* 2:1. The explanation I've given here is a basic outline, but there are many more questions and complexities dealt with in the traditional commentaries about the nature of the process and object here. The differing explanations are generated by the subtleties and ambiguities of phrasing in the original mishnaic and Talmudic sources. The explanation I give in the text is the one proposed by commentators such as Rashi and R. Yom Tov ben Avraham Asevilli (1250–1330), known by the acronym "Ritva." Once again, it is easy to get entangled in the serpentine arguments.

10   Fisch, *Rational Rabbis*, 69 ff.

11   In his *ha-Torah ve-ha-Mitzvah*, commenting on the beginning of *Parashat Hukkat* Numbers 19, Malbim also senses something far more profound at stake here than one oven, or the status of legal authority. The Sages, he says, speak in riddles. I briefly summarize only a few points of his interpretation as follows. He connects the philosophical meanings of *tumah* and *taharah*, the ritual of the red heifer, and the dispute over the Akhnai oven, to the broader debates between the two leading schools of interpretation of the first century CE, Beit Shammai and Beit Hillel. The Talmud records hundreds of disputes between these two competing streams of interpretation of the Oral Law.

Malbim reminds us that the school of Shammai was far stricter in its notion of how much one could and should separate from material matters and the life of the flesh, in order to be "pure" in this world. A person, he writes, is also metaphorically compared to clay pottery in the Torah. The Oral Law specifies that clay pottery that has become *tame'* needs first to be broken, and then reconstructed till it is a whole vessel. A dead body is one of the principal causes of ritual impurity, but when the body dissolves into earth it is purified, since earth cannot contract *tumah*. One who ascetically "kills himself when alive," to use Malbim's words (i.e., breaks his body while alive) is like the oven of Akhnai, undergoing purification. But the question is: To what extent is that practical, advisable, or admirable in this world?

The school of Hillel argued that such stripping of the soul from the body is neither possible nor advisable in this world. One is always susceptible to *tumah* in this finite earthly life; one can't be completely pure. One should not strive to leave the world, or exceed the boundaries the Torah itself has given. Only in the next world is it possible to attain a level of complete purity. R. Eliezer was following the views of Beit Shammai here versus the Sages who were following Beit Hillel.

Though this reading makes the clay vessel or oven a kind of metaphor, it connects the story to serious theological debates occurring during the historical period of R. Eliezer and his colleagues.

12   R. Yosef Eliyahu Henkin *"Malkhut Yisrael, Medinat Yisrael, ve-Torat Yisrael"* in *ha-Darom* 29 (Nissan 5729) [1969]: 4. [Translation mine].

13   The Jerusalem Talmud, in a famous passage, notes that R. Akiva was a supporter of Bar Kokhba's rebellion (Jer. Talmud *Ta'anit* 4:8) and thought Bar Kokhba was the Messiah but later was shown to be wrong. R. Henkin thinks R. Akiva's bitter weeping at R. Eliezer's funeral is a sign of his remorse after R. Akiva, too, recognizes the disastrous consequences of that support. But by then it is too late. Henkin also accounts for the other details of the story and the meanings of the various miracles R. Eliezer performs.

14   In an e-mail to me from December 26, 2009, Robert Eisen notes a possible powerful intra-textual connection between the "snake" of "The Oven of Akhnai" argument and the image of the snake wrapped around a jar in the story of the siege of Jerusalem in *Gittin* 56b. In the latter text, the snake represents the Jewish rebels, and the jar represents Jerusalem. In the dialogue between R. Yohanan and Vespasian, when R. Yohanan correctly predicts Vespasian's impending appointment as the next Emperor, Vespasian asks him, if he was a King, why didn't R. Yohanan come to him before? That is, sue for peace. R. Yohanan answers, "The *biryoni* among us did not let me." The text continues:

> He [Vespasian] said to him: "If there is a jar of honey around which a serpent is wound, would they not break the jar to get rid of the serpent?" [That is to say, they should break down the walls to get rid of the rebels]. He could give no answer. R. Yosef, or as some say R. Akiva, applied to him the verse, "[God] turns wise men backward and makes their knowledge foolish" [Isa. 44:25]. He ought to have said to him, "We take a pair of tongs and grip the snake and kill it, and leave the jar intact." [That is to say, we were waiting for an opportunity to get rid of them.] (*Gittin* 56b)

15   The interpretive circularity of the story links it to the snake image and to the famous "hermeneutic circle" of philosophy. Tzvi Bekerman and Yair Neuman express these connections in the following quotation:

Clearly the story could have been rendered otherwise, but the choice of the Talmudic editors points at their preference to emphasize two intermingled levels of interpretation. The first level is the interpretation of the Jewish law concerning a specific case. The second level is an interpretation of the interpretation process. These are the communicative and the meta-communicative levels Bateson saw as necessary and complementary aspects of any communication process (Bateson, 1973). The relation between the levels is recursive. Not the empirical, nor the ideal, nor the interpretative will do. The Sages' decision is based on a scholarly consensus that receives its authority from the interpretative framework God instructed the Sages to use. The validity of the interpretation is derived from a given interpretative framework (the whole). At the same time, the interpretative framework receives its power from the community (the Sages) who adopt it as their own. This is the point at which the notion of the hermeneutic circle, the *ourobouros* (the legendary snake that bites its own tail), and many other forms of circularity and recursion come to mind.

Bekerman and Neuman, "Provocative Idea: On Borges' Amnesia and Talmudic Understanding: Reviving Ancient Traditions," *Journal of Research Practice* 1, no.1 (2005): 1.

Jeffrey Rubenstein also draws attention to Daniel Boyarin's *Intertextuality and the Reading of Midrash* (Bloomington, IN: Indiana University Press, 1990). Boyarin observes that the way the story makes the point adds another layer to the paradox:

> The proof texts cited by R. Yehoshua and R. Yirmiah . . . have different and opposite meanings in their original contexts. Deut. 30:12 and Exod. 23:22 are interpreted by the Sages to give themselves the authority to overrule the divine will. The Sages' claim to interpretive authority, then ultimately depends on the very interpretive authority that it claims. (35–36)

16 Rubenstein, *Talmudic Stories* (Baltimore: Johns Hopkins University Press, 1999): 40–41.

17 Traditional rabbinic commentaries to the story through the centuries also offer many interpretations of what the uprooted carob tree, backwards flowing stream and tottering walls of the study house symbolize, but I have no space here to expound at length on these aspects of the story.

18 Interestingly, the Jerusalem Talmud's version of this story puts it in the context of the laws of *niddui* (banning) in tractate *Mo'ed Katan*. For a thorough examination, see Michelle Hammer-Kossoy's dissertation on these forms of rabbinic punishment and their origins, "Divine Justice in Rabbinic Hands: Talmudic Reconstruction of the Penal System," (PhD. diss., New York University, September 2005). See especially pages 521–54 on *niddui* and *herem* (excommunication). Radal's, (R. David Luria) introduction to *Pirkei de-Rabbi Eliezer* has an extensive

set of interesting arguments about this issue, with Radal maintaining the position that it was *niddui* versus Nachmanides' position that it was *herem.*

19   Daniel J.H. Greenwood, "Akhnai: Legal Responsibility in the World of the Silent God," *Utah Law Review* (1997): 25. http://papers.ssrn.com/sol3/papers. cfm?abstract_id=794784.

20   Ibid., 33.

21   R. Yehudah Amital. "The Simple Sound of Truth," based on an oral discourse adapted by Aviad Hacohen and translated by Karen Fish. *The Israel Koschitsky Virtual Beit Midrash,* http://www.vbm-torah.org/roshandyk/rh63-rya.htm.

R. Marc Kujavski further connects the legal issue of the oven to these larger metaphysical issues. Read this way, the conflict at base is not one of a more democratic and pluralistic hermeneutic versus a conservative one. Behind it lies a more fundamental theological debate about the nature of the world, its relation to the Creator, and the ways in which the infinite and finite interact. I here add some further remarks to the explanation in note 8 above. This is my understanding of ideas taken from R. Kujavski's seminar on kabbalistic understandings of the first verses of Genesis, given in Jerusalem, July, 2010.

I am not able to go into the lengthy background required to fully clarify these points. To simplify a complex idea, however, kabbalistic tradition tries to solve the question of how, given God's infinity and all-encompassing presence, there can be "space" for a finite world. (This issue parallels the classical Greek philosophical problem of "the One and the Many.") The kabbalistic innovation is the idea of God's original "contraction" or *tzimtzum,* of His infinite Light. Creation occurs first not by expansion but by contraction. This movement of God's *tzimtzum* creates a "vessel" or form that can "contain" the divine creative light, and so enable the birth of a finite world that can endure as such. Without such a contraction, the finite would be obliterated in the infinite, the world unable to endure—just as a tsunami of water that sweeps away all in its path. (For a pedagogical application of this idea of the teacher's need to "contract" her- or himself to make a place for the student and enable the student to absorb the knowledge, see my essay "Knowledge Has a Face.") So there needs to be boundaries, containers, limits.

But how strictly then do these "vessels," these "containers," these forms resulting from the contraction, separate God and the world, infinite and finite? Do the vessels still somehow connect *directly* to and *reflect* the infinite Source above? Are there "openings" in the vessels that allow for direct flow between above and below, and a place for the infinite in the finite? Or are these vessels opaque, closed. If so, the finite world would be very distant from its Source, disconnected and diminished.

What does the interpretation of Torah and our Akhnai oven have to do with all this? When we understand "vessel" as a conceptual and metaphysical category, the specific legal and larger theological issues of the story unite. We remember from the Mishnah, that only a complete vessel can be susceptible to *tumah* (impurity); one that is broken or incomplete is not susceptible to *tumah.*

The Sages claim that the Akhnai oven is "complete," "closed," and thus suscepti-ble to *tumah*; R. Eliezer says it is not complete, and thus *tahor* (pure). Now both the oven and the Torah have the status of "vessels"—the Torah itself is a "vessel" mediating heaven and earth, infinite and finite. The question is: to what extent does it, and must it, directly connect to and reflect Heaven. And especially after the catastrophes of the Temple's destruction, how is it to be interpreted, adapted, opened, or closed? R. Yehoshua, in response to R. Eliezer's arguments, traditions, and supernatural proofs, finally retorts in the climactic moment of the story that the Torah "is not in heaven!"; one has to follow the majority vote on the issue. As R. Kujavski phrases it in his lecture, the debate is about "Whether a Torah that 'is not in heaven,' is still the Torah of God?" In other words, what kind of vessel is it? In what way do the infinite and finite, God and the world, connect? R. Eliezer's position, as opposed to R. Yehoshua, is that only the Torah that is connected directly to its divine Source, is a Godly Torah.

I hope my summary explanation is not too cryptic, but I take the risk, since this is another level of explaining why the argument between R. Eliezer and the Sages was about this particular legal question of the oven, and how that seemingly minor issue reflected critical differences in the views of the Sages about the nature of Torah, God and the world—so much so that it engendered R. Eliezer's intense opposition, and the Sages' consequent ban. And it helps clarify why R. Eliezer does not recant, but adheres to his position until the moment of his death, and dies with the word "*tahor*" on his lips, as we will see in chapter 3.

22 R. Tzadok Ha-Kohen, *Tzidkat ha-Tzaddik*, 64. [Translation mine].

23 R. Chaim Miller notes that the Jewish mystics trace the differing interpretations of the Talmudic Rabbis to the spiritual source or level of each Rabbi's soul and the way each "gazed" at the spiritual source of the Torah in the "higher" worlds. Talmudic debate refracts and processes that "gaze" through exacting forms of Talmudic and human logic, and the final legal decisions become contingent upon time and place as well. There is an interesting compilation in English of kabbalistic and Hasidic sources on the relation of various spiritual worlds to Tal-mudic debates, and specifically to "The Oven of Akhnai" story, in *Rambam: The Thirteen Principles of Faith: Principles VIII and IX*, ed. Chaim Miller (Brooklyn: Kol Menachem, 2007), 48–61 and 115–25, from which I adapted the sentences of this paragraph and those below.

As Miller further notes, though, in Jewish law, one can't make a ruling on the basis of prophecy. The argument has to stand based on the logic of the earthly Talmudic system as well. In his summary of the Akhnai story, based on the writings of the late Lubavitcher Rebbe, R. Menachem M. Schneersohn (d. 1994), when R. Eliezer says "Let heaven *prove* it," he means let heaven *prove* which rational argument is correct. And since the heavenly voice declares that the law is according to R. Eliezer, the Rabbis need to rethink their proofs. But if the other Sages still cannot rationally agree, and are unable to make the heavenly and the earthly decisions fit together, then the *worldly* view ultimately prevails.

Yet a large question remains: If R. Eliezer's point of view emanated from a higher level of truth, from a higher "world"—and was a greater revelation than his colleagues could contain, what would be his mistake? It would be, argues R. Schneersohn, that he nevertheless pressed them, and they had to rule in favor of a lesser revelation though they knew it did not represent the highest level of truth. While I do not have space here to enter further into the intricacies of Kabbalah or Hasidic thinking, from this perspective R. Eliezer would be arguing for the law as seen and refracted through a higher spiritual world than that of R. Yehoshua and his colleagues. I would add that perhaps this is something analogous to the difference between what is called in kabbalistic sources the world of *nekudim*, a world where the root and being of each thing is an absolute independent unity, complete in itself, as opposed to the next, lower world of *atzilut*, where the being of things is in the interrelation of their parts. This distinction between *nekudim* and *atzilut* is found in R. Moshe Hayyim Luzzatto's (Ramhal), *KL"H [138] Pithei Hokhmah*, ch. 39–40.) Thus we could extrapolate that for the Sages, the parts of the oven glued together do interconnect and comprise a real whole (*atzilut* perspective) or a complete vessel, but for R. Eliezer they do not; each remains independent (*nekudim* perspective).

24 An interesting source in the Talmud, *Niddah* 7b, discusses differences of opinion between R. Eliezer and R. Yehoshua about some other technical laws of *tumah* and *taharah* and adds:

> It was taught: R. Eliezer said to R. Yehoshua, "You have not heard, but I have heard; you have only heard one tradition but I have heard. Many people do not ask him who has not seen the new moon to come and give evidence, but only him who has seen it" [Witnesses were required to verify the appearance of the new moon each month and the Jewish lunar calendar was set accordingly]. Throughout the lifetime of R. Eliezer the people acted in accordance with the ruling of R. Yehoshua, but after the passing away of R. Eliezer, R. Yehoshua re-introduced the earlier practice [of R. Eliezer]. Why did he not follow R. Eliezer during his lifetime?—Because R. Eliezer was a disciple of Shammai [*shamuti*] and he felt that if they would act in agreement with his ruling in one matter, they would act in agreement with his rulings in other matters also, and that out of respect for R. Eliezer no one could interfere with them. But after the passing away of R. Eliezer, when the people could well be interfered with, he re-introduced the original practice.

Some classical commentators, such as Rashi, understand the meaning of *shamuti* to be "one placed under the ban"; others, such as R. Ya'akov ben Meir, known as "Rabbenu Tam" (1100–1171), take it to mean "a follower of the School of Beit Shammai." In general, when Beit Hillel differs from Beit Shammai, the law, with some exceptions, follows Beit Hillel.

25 A popular oral teaching often attributed to both R. Joseph B. Soloveitchik and R. Hayyim Shmuelevitz. In an email message from July, 2009, R. Jeffrey Saks

brought to my attention that the *Sefer ha-Hinnukh*, a classic Jewish medieval treatise on the 613 commandments (here Mitzvah #496), suggests that R. Eliezer indeed possessed the truth, as proclaimed by the "voice from heaven" (*bat kol*). This treatise argues that in this complex debate, his colleagues could not fathom the depths of his opinion and they did not want to agree to his words, even after the *bat kol* affirmed his correctness. So they cited a proof from the biblical law that one has to follow, "incline," after the majority opinion—whether it is truth or whether it might be mistaken. And *that* was what God was reacting to in saying *nitzhuni banai*, "My sons have defeated me." They inclined away from the path of truth that R. Eliezer intended, but they had the power of the commandment of the Torah itself to always follow the majority opinion in legal decision. So it was necessary, in this case, to agree with them, even if the truth was lacking, but such agreement would be considered "as if" the master of truth triumphed. R. Saks interprets this comment to signify a conflict between "objective truth" (R. Eliezer and the heavenly voice) and another type of "methodological or systemic truth" (the Sages); inherent in the Torah system is the preference for the latter.

26   Greenwood, "Akhnai," 33–34. As mentioned above, the Akhnai story continues to inspire passions and endless commentary today. There are pages and pages of lively responses and counter-responses to it on the Hebrew internet website, www.hydepark.hevre.co.il. Not all these, of course, are informed by the most sound scholarship, but creative interpretations still abound. One of the writers suggests that in its context and at the finale, "It is not in heaven" means that there is a responsibility of human beings to care for the continuation of the world and mend it ethically and spiritually. Imma Shalom was sensitive to this, and tried to prevent her husband's wounded feelings from having further disastrous consequences but failed. The walls of the study house, as the story says, are still inclined, to this day—in danger of falling at any moment. Their direction and support depend on us and the way we relate to each other in the study hall and outside it. Jeffrey Rubenstein discusses the role of honor and shame in Talmudic culture and the *beit midrash* from a more academic, critical and literary perspective in his various books on rabbinic stories.

Chapter 3

1   For other analyses of this story, see especially Alon Goshen-Gottstein's perceptive essay in Hebrew, "Hakham Boded al Eres Devai: Sippur Mitat Rabbi Eliezer—Nittuah Ideologi," in *Mehkarim be-Talmud u-ve-Midrash: Sefer Zikkaron le-Tirtzah Lifschitz*, ed. Moshe bar Asher et al. (Jerusalem: Mossad Bialik, 2005), 79–112. I also thank Jeffrey Rubenstein for generously sharing his forthcoming work on this story with me. Among standard earlier academic and less literary analyses of the story are those of Jacob Neusner, *Eliezer ben Hyrcanus: The Tradition and the Man* (Leiden: Brill, 1973) and Yitzhak Gilat, *R. Eliezer ben Hyrcanus: A Scholar Outcast* (Ramat-Gan: Bar-Ilan University Press, 1984).

2   Emmanuel Levinas, "Desacralization and Disenchantment," *Nine Talmudic Readings*, ed. and trans. Annette Aronowicz (Bloomington, IN: Indiana University Press, 1994), 142.

3   See also the parallel source in *Avot de-Rabbi Natan [Nussah alef]* ch. 25, 80; see Babylonian Talmud, *Sanhedrin* 101a; *Avot de-Rabbi Natan* [A] ch. 19, 70. Yonah Fraenkel's excellent literary analysis of the shorter version of this story in the Jerusalem Talmud, "Ha-Zeman ve-ha-Itzuv," is found in the collection of his essays, *Sippur ha-Aggadah: Ahdut shel Tokhen ve-Tzurah* (Tel Aviv: Ha-Kibbutz Ha-Me'uhad, 2001), 156–63. Fraenkel cautions that his insights should not be transferred from the version of the story in the Jerusalem Talmud to the longer account in the Babylonian Talmud. But I think there are certain parallels where it indeed can be applied. His sense of the time elements and tensions in the story strongly influences my reading.

4   The Talmud *Menahot* 36b discusses the issue. R. Akiva derives the exclusion of wearing tefillin on the Sabbath and Jewish holidays from the biblical verse that refers to tefillin as an "*ot*" (sign): "And it shall be for you a sign on your arm and a remembrance between your eyes so that the word of God be in your mouth, for God took you out of Egypt with a strong arm" (Exod. 13:9). Exodus 31:17 also refers to Shabbat as an "*ot*." Both are signs of the deep connection of God and Israel, and so on the Sabbath, a second "sign" would be superfluous. But why does R. Eliezer insist on still wearing his tefillin? Today, tefillin are generally worn only during prayer, but in earlier eras, especially among exceptional individuals, they were worn all day as a sign of special holiness, purity, and intense attachment to God . . . except on the Sabbath day. Perhaps R. Eliezer does not want to be stripped of them, since this would symbolize his soon being stripped of everything as he leaves the world. (Many Jewish men through history have saved and clung to their tefillin when all else was physically lost to them.) He has already been stripped of his position as teacher and rabbinic authority. This may be the last shred of his dignity. Whatever the motive, on a literary level, the effect of the image of R. Eliezer enwrapped in tefillin enshrouds him with purity.

5   The phrase is used just a handful of times in the vast Talmudic corpus, so the repetitions and echoes in these stories appear to me to be especially significant. Ironically, I find myself using the same phrase, "appear to me" in the preceding sentence to make my own statement here— rhetorically asserting and qualifying at once, hedging my bets.

6   Fraenkel, "Ha-Zeman ve-ha-Itzuv," 161.

7   For example, see "Ben Ish Hai," Yosef Hayyim ben Eliyahu al-Hakham, *Sefer Ben Yehoyada*, on *Sanhedrin* 67–68, ch. 7 s.v. "Lo haya lanu penai"; and "Nikhnesu ve-yishvu le-fanav me-rahok daled amot": "It seems that just as it is permitted to lie (*le-shannot*) for the sake of [preserving peace], so it is permitted to lie to [preserve] honor, since it was not polite to tell him that they had not come because they had banned him."

8   For a thorough examination of the practice of *niddui* in rabbinic law and its relation to other rabbinic punishments such as *herem* (ostracism) and for further

discussion of this story, see Michelle Hammer-Kossoy's dissertation, "Divine Justice in Rabbinic Hands: Talmudic Reconstruction of the Penal System," (PhD. diss., New York University, September 2005), 418–548.

9   In a well-known parable, R. Akiva explains why he is still teaching Torah publicly though it has been forbidden by the Roman government on pain of death. The parable is that of a fox who craftily attempts to lead the fish out of the water to escape the fishermen's nets. But just as the fish can't live outside the water, Israel can't live without the Torah. So in other words, if R. Akiva continues to teach he is going to die; but if he doesn't teach he will also die (*Berakhot* 61b).

10   R. Eliyahu Yosef Henkin, "Malkhut Yisrael, Medinat Yisrael, ve-Torat Yisrael," *Ha-Darom*, vol. 23 (Nissan, 5729 [1968]): 5.

11   For example, a midrash in *Ketubbot* 111a describes the famous "oaths" that God makes Israel and the nations of the world swear. This passage interprets verses in the Songs of Songs (2:7, 3:5, and 5:8) to mean that Israel has taken two oaths: (1) not to "storm the wall," i.e., forcefully return en masse from exile to the Land of Israel; and (2) not to rebel against the nations of the world. The nations of the world also vow that they will not oppress Israel too much.

12   Robert Alter, *The Art of Biblical Narrative* (New York: Basic books, 1981), 12, 87.

13   Haym Soloveitchik's now famous article, "Rupture and Reconstruction: The Transformation of Contemporary Orthodoxy," *Tradition* 28 (1994): 64–130 deals with a somewhat similar phenomenon in the way Jewish law is studied and applied in the contemporary Orthodox world. He delineates the difference between traditional "mimetic" knowledge gained through personal relation to oral traditions and living exemplars, and knowledge gained only from texts, from written instructions.

14   R. Jeffrey Saks, e-mail to the author, July 20, 2009.

15   Ben Ish Hai, *Sefer Ben Yehoyada*, s.v. "U-mah she-heniah zero'otav."

16   See also the direct identification of R. Eliezer with a Sefer Torah in *Sotah* 49b where it is said, "When R. Eliezer died, the Sefer Torah was hidden away [*nignaz*]"—meaning he personified it. Rashi, commenting there, refers to our scene in *Sanhedrin* 68a and to R. Eliezer as a master of halakhic traditions. See also another version of the Sages visiting him when ill in *Sanhedrin* 101a and the Sages crying, "Shall the Scroll of the Torah [i.e., R. Eliezer] lie in pain, and we not weep?"

On the Sage as embodied Torah, see especially Martin Jaffee, "A Rabbinic Ontology of the Written and Spoken Word: On Discipleship, Transformative Knowledge, and the Living Texts of Oral Torah," *Journal of the American Academy of Religion* 65:3 (1997): 526–49. Jaffee analyzes the way in which the Oral Torah is transmitted in face-to-face encounters between rabbinic Sages and their students in what Jaffee calls a "system of discipleship." He defines the latter as one wherein "the teacher bears for each student a responsibility appropriate to that of kin" (530), and the disciple absorbs the teaching of the Sage "in such a way as to embody the teacher's 'own human achievement'" (530). The Sage was also meant to embody the Torah and in this sense was also a "Text" (538), a "living text." Accordingly, even the text of the Written Torah "fulfills the telos of its being only when its code is lifted by the Sage's voice off the written scroll and incorporated into the Oral Torah of his own life" (541). "Discipleship was the process that enabled one to read as texts the highly coded behaviors of Sages and, in turn, to compose texts with ones' own life that others might themselves learn to read" (543). See also the extensive analysis by R. Joseph B. Soloveitchik, in his essay "Ha-Yehudi Mashul le-Sefer Torah" in *Beit Yosef Shaul: Kovetz Hiddushei Torah* (New York: Gruss Kollel, Yeshiva University, 1994), 68–100 about the likening of *every* Jew to a Sefer Torah, not as simply a lovely metaphor but as what he calls a fundamental "axiom" in Jewish legal and philosophical thought.

17 The text is grammatically somewhat awkward. The verb used here is "*hesarti*." "*Hesir*" would roughly translate as "abstracted" or "skimmed" but more literally means "to lessen, diminish, deduct, subtract." In other words, R. Eliezer was only able to take a tiny portion of what he learned from his teachers, due to the vastness of their knowledge. He "reduced" or "subtracted" from that great amount only a bit. But the line could be read also to mean he did not *even* subtract a small amount, from their overflowing sea . . . whatever he took still left an overwhelming amount. Hence some of the classical commentators read it as "diminishing the ratio" of the teacher's knowledge to the students. There is both an emended and unamended version of Rashi, one of the most authoritative traditional medieval commentators. The emended version reads that despite "all my students learned from me, they reduced the ratio of my knowledge to theirs only as much as the level of eye-powder in a tube is reduced through one dip of the applicator." The unamended version has R. Eliezer saying that he *did* diminish his teacher's knowledge as much as a dog laps from the sea but his students *did not* diminish his as much as applicator dipped in tube of eye powder. See also the commentary of Maharsha on this line.

18 Levinas, "Desacralization and Disenchantment," 156.

19 Ben Ish Hai, *Sefer Ben Yehoyada* s.v., "Harbeh Torah lamadti."

20 Levinas, "Desacralization and Disenchantment," 142.

21 Michael Chabon, *The Amazing Adventures of Kavalier & Clay* (New York: Picador, 2000), 359.

22 R. Joseph B. Soloveitchik, *Halakhic Man*, trans. Lawrence Kaplan (Philadelphia, JPS: 1983), 73. See also pages 36–37 for another description of his grandfather's watching a beautiful sunrise and at the same time feeling an overwhelming melancholy, thinking of the finality of death. R. Soloveitchik comments on the relation of the aesthetic experience and the tragic sense of mortality: for "halakhic man," communication with the Creator and redemption do not come through escape into transcendent mysterious realms "but via the world itself, by the adaption and dedication of the empirical reality to the ideal patterns of *halakha*."

23 Levinas, "Desacralization and Disenchantment," 141.

24 Ibid., 153.

25 Ibid., 152.

26   Ibid., 145. This "purity" of the Pharisees, Levinas continues, is not "inner purity" in the classical Western or Christian sense—which Levinas sees as another kind of "magic." In his sharp polemic against that kind of religious sensibility, Levinas supports the need for the Sages to employ external criteria when discussing laws of ritual purity: "These rules of the external gesture must be there for inner purity to stop being merely verbal." Otherwise purity becomes so "spiritual-ized" that "it risks making us drown in nihilist abysses of interiority in which pure and impure become identified with each other" ("Descaralization and Disenchantment," 153). So, in his view, these rabbinic rules and external gestures connect the physical and spiritual without allegorizing them, without enacting a bewitching sorcery. See also the discussion of Levinas in my book, *Fragments of Redemption: Jewish Thought and Literary Theory in Scholem, Benjamin, and Levinas*, (Bloomington, IN: Indiana University Press, 1992).

For a different view of the relation of "the holy" to the "sacred," and the dif-ference between Jewish versions of "holiness" and classical academic scholarly misreading of the "sacred" by modern scholars such as Rudolf Otto and Mircea Eliade, see Moshe Idel: "*Ganz Andere*: On Rudolph Otto and Concepts of Holi-ness in Jewish Mysticism," *Da'at: A Journal of Jewish Philosophy and Kabbalah* 57–59 (2006): 5–44. Idel notes that *kedushah*, "holiness" in Jewish texts, can signify "absolutely other"—but in both rabbinic and kabbalistic texts, it can also signify a moment of intensely *bringing close*—of community between God and humanity. This can occur not just in mystical experiences but in the most ordinary realms—in blessings, prayers, sexuality. "Holiness" can have a transi-tive meaning as well, as in the Hebrew word for marriage: "*kiddushin.*" I think Levinas, coming from a Lithuanian, rationalistic Jewish background, misses this important aspect. The line between loving mutual influence and attempt-ing manipulation and arousal of divine forces can be a thin one . . . as it is in any love relationship.

27   Askénazi, *La Parole et l'écrit: Penser la tradition juive aujourd'hui*, vol. 2, ed. Marcel Goldmann (Paris: Albin Michel, 2005), 266–73.

28   Chabon, *Kavalier & Clay*, 582.

29   I am grateful to Simi Peters for this insight shared in an oral conversation from June, 2008 in a discussion of *Sanhedrin* 68a.

30   Kenneth Burke, "Perspective by Incongruity: Comic Correctives," in *On Symbols and Society*, ed. Joseph R. Gusfield, (Chicago: University of Chicago Press, 1989), 261 ff.

31   Mishnah *Kelim* 23:1 discusses this issue.

32   Chabon, *Kavalier & Clay*, 359.

33   Ora Wiskind-Elper, e-mail to the author, March 1, 2009.

34   David Katzin further relates the outside/inside issue in our story to *Berakhot* 27b-28a where we find that Rabban Gamaliel himself is the target of a kind of "ban"; he is temporarily overthrown as the head of the academy at Yavneh:

Here too the argument was about one thing . . . evening prayer. . . . But the story is about many other things as well. In this case Rabban Gamaliel feels that one's interior (in this case character) must be as impeccable as his exterior façade to study Torah. The Sages felt this was too strict and added 400 and 700 new benches to the study hall. Rabban Gamaliel is alarmed and wonders if he has withheld Torah from Israel. He "was shown in a dream" white casks filled with ashes. The exterior covers a problematic interior. In this case, we are told the imagery meant nothing; rather it was given to appease Rabban Gamaliel. Is seeing a parallel between Rabban Gamaliel's casks and R. Eliezer's oven the result of an overactive imagination or were such allusions a symbol of the complaint of the older generations against the new? (E-mail to the author, March 29, 2009)

Menachem Fisch's analysis of the oven of Akhnai story would somewhat support this hunch. He argues that the words in the story *"On that day (bo ba-yom)* R. Eliezer brought forth every imaginable argument"* indicate to the well-informed reader that the story is directly related to the overthrow of Rabban Gamaliel in the rebellion in the academy narrated in *Berakhot* 27b–28a. He was replaced with the younger R. Eleazar ben Azariah who presided over "anti-traditionalist" reforms. *Berakhot* 28a says:

> They taught Testimonies [*Eduyyot*] that day. And anywhere wherever the expression "on that day" [*bo ba-yom*] is used [in the Mishnah], it refers to that day. And there was not a single law [*halakhah*] about which any doubt existed in the Beit ha-Midrash which was not fully elucidated.

In other words, "on that day"—the big day—all unresolved halakhic issues were decided, and those who taught them came to testify to their traditions in the face of a majority now empowered to vote them down. The oven of Akhnai is listed in the Mishnah *Eduyyot* 7:7 and Tosefta *Eduyyot* 2:1 as one of many testimonies and cases presented and voted "on that day" at Yavneh. See Fisch's *Rational Rabbis*, 65–81. I have simplified Fisch's rich analysis for the sake of space. See also the analysis of *Berakhot* 27b–28a by Jeffrey Rubenstein in his *Stories of the Babylonian Talmud*, 77–90, for a good summary of the academic discussion about the story, the literary issues involved, and the scholarship pertaining to it.

35 Eliezer Segal notes this possible connection of the shoe to the person of R. Eliezer in the law discussed in the text, but has doubts the editors intend it to be anything more than a halakhic discussion. His perspective is historical-critical. Mine is literary, and as a literary critic I am also more skeptical about notions of one-dimensional "authors' intentions" and how we can know them. Regardless, the *rhetorical effect* of the text on the reader powerfully links the person of R. Eliezer to the seemingly arcane, legal topic, as does the context. See Eliezar Segal, "Law as Allegory? An Unnoticed Literary Device in Talmudic Narratives," *Prooftexts* 8 (1988): 245–56.

Alan Goshen-Gottstein, in his analysis, reads the last scene as I do. Yardena

Cope-Yosef also sees the image of the shoe as significant: "the shoe attached to this world–the interface that did not work too well for R. Eliezer . . . " E-mail to the author, June 6, 2006.

36 T.S. Eliot, *Selected Essays* (London: Faber and Faber, 1951), 144–45.

37 Ora Wiskind-Elper further notes:

> In effect, this is the terrible paradox of his story and the image of the shoe and the last. . . . The shoe—the body—becomes *tame'* when it is removed from the last—when it is separated from the soul. R. Eliezer resisted that separation of "inner" and "outer" until his final moment. When his soul leaves his body he is, finally, broken apart. But that moment, for the Sages, makes him into a *keli*, a vessel and *whole* according to their definition of the oven—and susceptible to *tumah* . . . .Breaking needs to be seen not only as a tragedy but as a terrible yet fruitful and vitally important experience. (E-mail to the author, March 1, 2009)

See also *Niddah* 7b stating that after R. Eliezer's passing, R. Yehoshua reinstituted earlier practices that followed R. Eliezer's opinion, over which they had debated and disagreed in R. Eliezer's lifetime.

38 See chapter 2, note 11 for the importance of issues of purity in rabbinic traditions.

39 The Jewish mystical tradition engages in many efforts to realign and reunite heaven and earth. The *Zohar* is one of the classics of Jewish mysticism which tradition ascribes to R. Shimon bar Yohai, who was the prime student of R. Akiva. Academic scholars estimate that it was edited and redacted in the twelfth century. The *Zohar* rewrites the story of R. Eliezer's passing from a mystical perspective in the *Midrash ha-Ne'elam, Zohar* I, 98a-99a. In this version, R. Eliezer reveals profound mysteries to his son and discourses with R. Akiva on the "mysteries of the Chariot," meaning Talmudic mystical speculation on the esoteric vision on Ezekiel, chapter 1. Fire comes from heaven to surround all the Sages gathered at his deathbed, and they discuss the mysteries of the biblical book the Song of Songs. R. Eliezer stretches his arms out and lays them on his heart and says: "Alas for the world, the upper world. You are about to take back and conceal all the light and illumination from the lower world." This version is an enchanting mystical midrash on the text in *Sanhedrin* 68a. I thank Melila Eshed-Hellner for this reference.

40 R. Askénazi further argues that after Cain's murder of Abel, this problematic is carried on through all the genealogies of the first few chapters of Genesis—the genealogy of Cain is opposed to that of the second son born to Adam and Eve, Seth. Seth's line is meant to correct what Abel was unable to do. Both Cain's line and Seth's line also give birth to figures called "*Hanokh*," from the Hebrew word meaning "to educate"; but these figures also fail. Seth's line culminates in Abraham, who is finally able to find the right balance between the two tendencies, heaven and earth, kindness and severity; he teaches humanity about the

One God and becomes the Father to many nations. The trajectory begins to rise again from Abraham to the future Messiah. History, then, as R. Askénazi puts it, is a "drama," but not a "tragedy." Askénazi, *Sod ha-Ivri: Yesodot ha-Emunah le-Or Pesukei ha-Torah*, vol. 1, trans. and ed. Gavriela ben Shmuel and Israel Pibko (Jerusalem: Hava Beit El, 2004), esp. 202–5.

41   R. Léon Askénazi, "L'option pharisienne du Judaisme," in *La Parole et l'écrit: Penser la vie juive aujourd'hui*, vol. 2, ed. Marcel Goldmann (Paris: Albin Michel, 2005), 273. R Askénazi notes that in this paragraph he is paraphrasing an idea of Rav Avraham Yitzhak Kook in the latter's *Orot ha-Kodesh*, vol. 3, 267.

42   Levinas, "Desacralization and Disenchantment," 159.

43   A well-known midrash relates:

> What was Rabbi Akiva like? A worker who goes out with his basket. He finds wheat; he puts it in. Barley; he puts it in. Spelt; he puts it in. Beans; he puts them in. Lentils; he puts them in. When he arrives home, he sorts out the wheat by itself, barley by itself, spelt by itself, beans by themselves, lentils by themselves. Thus did Rabbi Akiva, and arranged the Torah rings by rings. (*Avot de-Rabbi Natan* ch. 18; see also *Gittin* 67a).

> See also *Yevamot* 62b, where the death of thousands of R. Akiva's students is related (possibly during the Bar Kokhba rebellion). "The world remained desolate until Rabbi Akiva came to our Masters in the South and taught the Torah to them. These were Rabbi Meir, Rabbi Yehudah, Rabbi Yose, Rabbi Shimon and Rabbi Eleazar ben Shammua; and it was they who revived the Torah at that time."

44   Levinas, "Desacralization and Disenchantment," 159.

45   In relation to the whole theme of sorcery here, Robert Eisen suggested to me in an e-mail from December 26, 2009 that the Rabbis permit sorcery when it has no practical benefit because it is an activity in which the Rabbi imitates God himself. This conclusion is based on Moshe Idel's research on the golem legends. This use of sorcery was, Eisen writes, "a way of tapping into the divine powers by which God created the world, thereby affirming their faith in God's creative abilities in a performative manner . . . a similar attitude likely underlies these passages regarding use of magic." As long as it is used for religious purposes, or to imitate God—and not for practical purposes—using magic is legitimate. Eisen interestingly also connects the story of R. Eliezer's beginnings with the scene here: "Note that in the instance of Eliezer and the cucumbers, he's also using magic in order to perform the activity that his father did, and that he himself was being groomed for as a young man—i.e., farming. He uses magic to collect produce. The fact that this activity is mentioned at the end of R. Eliezer's life is therefore very significant. He is coming back full circle to the activity of his childhood, the material and earthly activity of farming produce. But the major difference here is that he comes back to that activity for religious purpose, as

one who now imitates God. He has come back to the activity of his childhood, but in a way that transforms it into something more meaningful."

Joshua Levinson has a different understanding of rabbinic uses of magic, based on different methodological assumptions in his article "Enchanting Rabbis: Contest Narratives between Rabbis and Magicians in Late Antiquity." The article has a good survey of scholarship on the topic and some comments about this story as well. *Jewish Quarterly Review* 100 (2010): 54–94.

See also Moshe Idel's, *Golem: Jewish Magical and Mystical Traditions on the Artificial Anthropoid* (Albany, NY: SUNY Press, 1990).

46   Sources for this idea are *Sefer va-Yahel Moshe* ([Dessau, 1691] 9 fol. 42b and 51a) and popularized in *Seder ha-Dorot; Mikdash Melekh* on *Zohar* ("Bereshit" 17a); *Va-Yahel Moshe* by R. Moshe Graf ([Zalkavi, 1714], 45b and 54a). It is frequently cited in Hasidic literature as well. Menachem Kallus, who directed me to those sources in an e-mail from July 12, 2009, adds that "the origin of the idea is Lurianic—based likely on the verse: *ve-ha-kohanim ha-leviyim benei tzadok*—that Levites will be Kohanim, i.e., that when the world will be repaired and redeemed, it will no longer require free grace [*hesed*] but will be able to function via God's attribute of strict judgment [*din*]. Thus Shammai, who represents *din*, will overrule Hillel, who represents *hesed* [kindness, leniency]."

Maharal of Prague in his commentary on the story of the oven of Akhnai in his *Hiddushei Aggadot*, vol. 3, s.v. "Ein mevi'in re'ayah min haruv" and "Ka'asher amar min ha-shamayim yohihu" interprets it somewhat the opposite. To simplify a very complex reading, he argues that the "heavenly voice" (*bat kol*) supporting R. Eliezer's legal opinions is on a *lower* spiritual level than the "Torah view" argued for by the Sages. It is not that the Torah, which prescribes "inclining after the majority," is "less" heavenly and more earthly and more human—as some modern academic commentators seeking "democratic," "anti-traditional," "pluralistic" perspectives in the text often argue—but the opposite! Torah itself is on a *higher* spiritual level than the heavenly voice; Torah comes from heaven, but is given at Sinai already—and is higher than the *bat kol*; it was transmitted orally in prophecy. The *bat kol* in fact, according to Maharal, is on a level "closer to man," as seen in other Talmudic stories, and can come to every person. It is more graspable, unlike prophecy. So in this reading R. Eliezer's view is *not* more "heavenly" than theirs; but the law follows him "in every place" according to a *bat kol* level "because it's closer to man." The problem was when he pitted his own view against the majority of the Sages, for the Torah prescribes "inclining after the majority" and is itself a higher spiritual level; so R. Yehoshua asserts that we do not listen to a *bat kol*, and the Torah itself takes precedence.

Epilogue

1   *Nefesh ha-Rav*, ed. Hershel Shachter (Jerusalem: Reishit Yerushalyim, 1994), 290–91.

2   R. Joseph B Soloveitchik, "On the Love of Torah and the Redemption of This

Generation's Soul" (*Al Ahavat ha-Torah u-Geulat Nefesh ha-Dor*) in *Divrei Hashkafah* (Jerusalem: WZO Department for Torah Education and Culture for the Diaspora, 992), 241–58. I use the translation here by David Derovan in *Spirituality Today* (Jerusalem: Jewish Values Education Institute, OU Israel Center, 2002), 11. This pamphlet, however, includes only selections of the original essay. The complete version of the essay first appeared in the Hebrew newspaper *ha-Do'ar*, New York, 1 Sivan 5720 [1960]. See R. Jeffrey Saks' excellent historical analysis of this piece, "'Be-Khol Derakhekha Da'ehu': Rabbi Joseph B. Soloveitchik and the Israeli Chief Rabbinate: Biographical Notes (1959–60)," *BDD* 17 (2006): 45–67.

3   In his own eulogy for R. Hayyim Heller, R. Soloveitchik writes of the dialectic between the adult and child in the great Torah scholar:

> The adult is too clever. Utility is his guiding light. The experience of God is unavailable to those approaching it with a businesslike attitude. Only the child can breach the boundaries that segregate the finite from the infinite. Only the child with his simple faith and fiery enthusiasm can make the miraculous leap into the bosom of God. . . .
>
> When it came to faith, the giants of Torah, the geniuses of Israel, became little children with all their ingenuousness, gracefulness, simplicity, their tremors of fear, their vivid experiences in their devotion to them. . . . The mature, the adults, are not capable of the all-embracing and all-penetrating outpouring of the soul. The most sublime crown we can give a great man sparkles with the gems of childhood.

"A Eulogy for R. Chaim Heller," in *Shiurei Ha Rav: A Conspectus of the Public Lectures of Rabbi Joseph B. Soloveitchik*, ed. Joseph Epstein (New York: Ktav, 1994), 63–64.

4   Soloveitchik, "On the Love of the Torah," trans. Derovan, 12.

5   *Midrash Tanhuma*, end of "Va-Et'hanen," ch. 6.

6   A passage in *Pirkei Avot* 4:12 relates "Rabbi Eleazar ben Shammua said: Let the honor of your disciple be as dear to you as your own; and the honor of your friend be as the reverence for your teacher; and the reverence for your teacher be as the reverence for Heaven." R. Eleazar ben Shammua is mentioned in *Yevamot* 62a as one of the four new students R. Akiva taught after the loss of thousands of his previous disciples. R. Akiva in that text, "travels to the south," away from the decimation the Romans have caused in Judea, and begins once more to "sow his seed." Through these four new students he "gives birth" again, makes the world fecund, and regenerates the Torah. His new students became the pillars and innovators for the next generation. They are among the most famous and important names in rabbinic tradition: R. Meir, R. Yehudah ha-Nasi, R. Yose, R. Shimon bar Yohai, and R. Eleazar ben Shammua.

R. Eleazar ben Shammua's statement here seems to place the honor of one's student at the bottom point of an ascending linear hierarchy: from student, to friend, to teacher. At the top, the student's honor for his or her teacher is like reverence for God. R. Aaron Kahn in an intriguing (and typically rabbinic) reading of this line writes that if the amount of honor due your teacher is equal to the reverence for God, then how could the teacher, in turn, be asked to give the same amount of honor [reverence for God] to her or his student? That is, "Let the honor of your student be as dear to you as *your own* [honor]?" So it means, says Kahn, something else: that the teacher is obligated to honor the student *not* in his or her role as "teacher to the student" but in another mode—in a role reversal of sorts, as "student to the teacher." For the teacher is also a "student of his student."

It is not, then, a simple hierarchy, but a complex reciprocity, a mutual dependence. To be the student of one's student is another way of the student's "making the teacher." The teacher, as Kahn puts it, "ascends and descends according to his students; when the student is not at his or her best level, the teacher is injured." Aaron Kahn, "'Hadrat ha-Melekh': Al ha-Zikkah ha-Hadadit shel Rav ve-Talmid," *Beit Yosef Shaul: Kovetz Hiddushei Torah*, ed. Elchanan Asher Adler (New York: Gruss Kollel, R.Yitzhak Elchanan Seminary, Yeshiva University, 1993), 356–68.

Maimonides in his classic compendium of Jewish Law, the *Mishneh Torah*, places this principle into the section on the "Laws of Torah Study":

> A teacher is a student of his students. Students add to the wisdom of their Rabbi, and open his heart. The Sages said that they learned more from their Rabbis than from their friends [*Ta'anit* 7a], but learned even more from their students. Just as a small candle can light a big one so a student sharpens his Rabbi's wits, by extracting from him his wisdom by means of questions. (5:13)

7   See also the famous interpretation of R. Nahman of Bratslav on this passage in his *Likkutei Moharan*, "va-Yehi pi shenayim," ch. 66.

8   Kahn, "Hadrat ha-Melekh," 358, 359–66, 368.

SELECTED BIBLIOGRAPHY

Alter, Robert. *The Art of Biblical Narrative*. New York: Basic Books, 1981.

Aberbach, Moshe. *Ha-Hinukh bi-Tekufat ha-Mishnah ve-ha-Talmud*. Jerusalem: Rubin Mass, 1982.

Adelman, Rachel. *The Return of the Repressed: Pirqe De-Rabbi Eliezer and the Pseudo-epigrapha*. Leiden: Brill, 2009.

Amital, R. Yehudah. "The Simple Sound of Truth." Translated by Karen Fish. *The Israel Koschitsky Virtual Beit Midrash*. http://www.vbm-torah.org/roshandyk/rh63-rya.htm.

Arendt, Hannah. *Between Past and Future: Eight Exercises in Political Thought*. New York: Penguin, 1961.

Assaf, Simha. *Mekorot le-Toledot ha-Hinnukh be-Yisra'el*. Edited by S. Slick. New York: Jewish Theological Seminary, 2001. Originally published Tel Aviv: Dvir, 1945–1950.

Askénazi, R. Yéhouda Leon (Manitou). *"Jacob Gordin, mon maître."* In *Jacob Gordin, Écrits: le renouveau de la pensée juive en France*, edited by Marcel Goldmann, 9–18. Paris: Albin Michel, 1995.

———. *Ki Mitsion: La calendrier hebraique*, vol. 2. Jerusalem: Foundation Manitou, 1999.

———. *Ki MiTsion: Notes sur la Paracha*, vol. 1. Jeursalem: Foundation Manitou 1997.

———. *"Morale et sainteté: Etude des Pirké-Avot—Ch. 1 Mishnah 1." Mayanot: Cours transcrits du Rav Léon Askénazi-Manitou*, no. 5. Jerusalem: Foundation Manitou, 1993.

———. *La Parole et l'écrit: Penser la tradition juive aujourd'hui*. Edited by Marcel Goldmann. Vol. 1 of *Penser la tradition juive aujourd'hui*. Paris: Albin Michel, 1999.

———. *La Parole et l'écrit: Penser la tradition juive aujourd'hui*. Edited by Marcel Goldmann. Vol. 2 of *Penser la vie juive aujourd'hui*. Paris: Albin Michel, 2005.

———. *Sod ha-Ivri: Yesodot ha-Emunah le-Or Pesukei ha-Torah*, vol. 1. Edited by Israel Pibko. Jerusalem: Beit El, 2005.

———. *Sod Midrash ha-Toledot*. Edited by Hayyim Rotenberg. Jerusalem: Hava Beit El, 2009.

Auerbach, Erich. "Odysseus' Scar." In *Mimesis: The Representations of Reality in Western Literature*, 3–23. Princeton: Princeton University Press, 1953.

Avot de-Rabbi Natan im Haggahot ha-Gra. Edited by Meir Etrog. Benei-Berak, n.p., 2000.

Babylonian Talmud. English translation. Edited by Isidore Epstein. New York: Soncino, 1938.

Bekerman, Zvi, and Yair Neuman. "Provocative Idea: On Borges' Amnesia and Talmudic Understanding: Reviving Ancient Traditions in Re-search." *Journal of Research Practice* 1, no.1 (2005): 1–11.

Ben Ish Hai (R. Yosef Hayyim ben Eliyahu al-Hakham). *Sefer Ben Yehoyada*. Edited by Yeshua ben David Salim. Jerusalem, n.p., 1998.

Benjamin, Walter. *Illuminations*. Edited by Hannah Arendt. 1955. Reprint, New York: Schocken, 1969.

Booth, Wayne. *The Vocation of a Teacher*. Chicago: University of Chicago Press, 1988.

Bokser, Ben-Zion. *Pharisaic Judaism in Transition: R. Eliezer the Great and Jewish Reconstruction After the War with Rome*. New York: Bloch, 1935.

Boyarin, Daniel. *Intertextuality and the Reading of Midrash*. Bloomington: Indiana University Press, 1990.

Buber, Martin. "The Education of Character." In *Between Man and Man*, 104–17. 1955. Reprint, New York: Macmillan, 1967.

Buchler, Adolf. "Learning and Teaching in the Open Air in Palestine." *Jewish Quarterly Review* 4 (1914): 485–91.

Bynum, Caroline Walker. *Holy Feast and Holy Fast: The Religious Significance of Food to Medieval Women*. Berkeley: University of California Press, 1987.

Copeland, Steven. "The Oral Reading Experience in Jewish Learning." *Studies in Jewish Education* 2 (1984): 193–211.

Delia, Mary Alice. "Killer English: Postmodern Theory and the High School Classroom." PhD. diss., University of Maryland, 1991.

Drazin, Nathan. *History of Jewish Education from 515 BCE to 220 CE*. Baltimore: Johns Hopkins University Press, 1940.

Eliot, T. S. *Selected Essays*. London: Faber and Faber, 1951.

Finkelstein, E., ed. *Sifrei al Sefer Devarim*. 3rd edition. New York: Jewish Theological Seminary, 1993.

Fraade, Steven. *From Tradition to Commentary: Torah and Its Interpretation in the Midrash Sifre to Deuteronomy*. Albany: SUNY Press, 1991.

Fox, Seymour, Israel Scheffler, and Daniel Marom. *Visions of Jewish Education*. Cambridge: Cambridge University Press, 2004.

Fraenkel, Yonah. "Moto shel Rabbi Eliezer." In *Sippur ha-Aggadah: Ahdut shel Tohen ve-Tzurah: Kovetz Mehkarim*, 156–73. Tel Aviv: Ha-Kibbutz ha-Me'uhad, 2001.

Gilat, Yitzhak, D. *R. Eliezer ben Hyrcanus: A Scholar Outcast*. Ramat-Gan: Bar-Ilan University Press, 1984.

Gallop, Jane, ed. *Pedagogy: The Question of Impersonation*. Bloomington: Indiana University Press, 1995.

Glatzer, Nahum. *Franz Rosenzweig: His Life and Thought*. New York: Schocken, 1953.

Goldin, Judah, trans. *The Fathers According to Rabbi Nathan*. 1955. Reprint, New York: Schocken, 1974.

Goodblatt, David M. *Rabbinic Instruction in Sasanian Babylonia*. Leiden: Brill, 1974.

Goshen-Gottstein, Alon. "Hakham Boded al Eres Devai: Sippur Mitat Rabbi Eliezer: Nittuah Ideologi." In *Mehkarim be-Talmud u-ve-Midrash. Sefer Zikkaron le-Tirtzah Lifschitz*, edited by Moshe Bar-Asher et al., 79–112. Jerusalem: Mosad Bialik, 2005.

Green, Yekutiel, ed. *Ha-Rav ve-ha-Talmid al-pi Mishlei Habad u-Midrashei Hazal*. Kefar Habad, n.p., 1986.

Greenwood, Daniel H. "Akhnai." *Utah Law Review* 309 (1997): 309–58.

Gross, Benjamin. "Moreh ve-Talmid." Unpublished manuscript.

Gutoff, Joshua, "The Necessary Outlaw: The Catastrophic Excommunication & Paradoxical Rehabilitation of Rabbi Eliezer Ben Hyrcanus." *Journal of Law and Religion* 2 (1994–1995): 733–48.

Halbertal, Moshe, and Tovah Halbertal. "The Yeshiva." In *Philosophers on Education: Historical Perspectives*, edited by Amélie Oksenberg Rorty, 458–69. London: Routledge, 1988.

Hammer-Kossoy, Michelle. "Divine Justice in Rabbinic Hands: Talmudic Reconstitution of the Penal System." PhD diss., New York University, 2005.

Handelman, Susan. "Crossing the Void: A Meditation on Postmodern Jewish Theological Renewal." In *Reviewing the Covenant: Eugene Borowitz and the Postmodern Renewal of Jewish Theology*, edited by Peter Ochs, 173–200. New York: SUNY Press, 2000.

———. "Dear Class." In *Essays in Quality Learning: Teachers' Reflections on Classroom Practices*, edited by Steven Selden, 17–32. College Park: University of Maryland, IBM Total Quality Learning Project, 1998.

———. "Emunah: The Craft of Faith." In *The Academy and the Possibility of Belief*, edited by M. L. Buley-Meissner, 85–104. New York: Hampton Press, 2000.

———. "'Find(ing) Yourself a Teacher': Opening the Discussion on Pedagogy at the Association for Jewish Studies Conference." *Association for Jewish Studies Newsletter* 45 (Spring 1995): 8–9.

———. *Fragments of Redemption: Jewish Thought and Literary Theory in Scholem, Benjamin, and Levinas*. Bloomington: Indiana University Press, 1991.

———. "'Go Down Moses': Teaching in the New M.A. in Gender Studies Program at Bar-Ilan University." *Nashim: A Journal of Jewish Women's Studies and Gender Studies* 5 (Fall, 2002): 213–30.

———. "'Knowledge Has a Face': The Jewish, the Personal, and the Pedagogical." In *Personal Effects: The Social Character of Scholarly Writing*, edited by David Bleich and Deborah Holdstein, 121–44. Logan: Utah State University Press, 2001.

———. "The Philosopher, the Rabbi, and the Rhetorician." *College English* 72, no. 6 (July 2010): 590–607.

———. *The Slayers of Moses: The Emergence of Rabbinic Interpretation in Modern Literary Theory*. Albany: SUNY Press, 1982.

———. "'Stopping the Heart': The Spiritual Search of Students and the Challenge to a Professor in an Undergraduate Literature Class." In *Religion, Scholarship and Higher Education: Perspectives, Models and Future Prospects,* edited by Andrea Sterk, 202–30. Notre Dame, IN: University of Notre Dame Press, 2001.

———. "The Torah of Criticism and the Criticism of Torah: Recuperating the Pedagogical Moment." *Journal of Religion* 74, no. 3 (1994): 356–71. Originally published in *Interpreting Judaism in a Postmodern Age,* edited by Steven Kepnes, 221–42. New York: New York University Press, 1996.

———. "'We Cleverly Avoided Talking about God': Personal and Pedagogical Reflections on Academia and Spirituality." *Courtyard: A Journal of Research and Thought in Jewish Education* 1, no. 1 (1999): 101–20.

———. "Women and the Study of the Torah in the Thought of the Lubavitcher Rebbe: A Halakhic Analysis." In *Jewish Legal Writings by Women,* edited by Micah Halperin and Channah Safrai, 142–77. Jerusalem: Urim Press, 1998.

Handelman, Susan, and Ora Wiskind Elper, eds. *Torah of the Mothers: Contemporary Jewish Women Read Classical Jewish Texts.* Jerusalem: Urim Press, 2000.

Handelman, Susan, and Jeffrey Saks, eds. *"Wisdom from All My Teachers": Challenges and Initiatives in Contemporary Torah Education.* Jerusalem: Urim Press, 2003.

Hellner-Eshed, Melila. *A River Flows from Eden: The Language of Mystical Experience in the Zohar.* Palo Alto, CA: Stanford University Press, 2009.

———. "Teacher-Disciple Relationships in Judaism." *Encyclopedia of Love in World Religions,* edited by Yehudit Kornberg Greenberg. Santa Barbara: ABC-CLIO Press, 2007.

Harris, Maria. *Women and Teaching: Themes for a Spirituality of Pedagogy.* New York: Paulist Press, 1988.

———. *Teaching and the Religious Imagination: An Essay in the Theology of Teaching.* San Francisco: Harper San Francisco, 1987.

Haskell, Ellen. "Metaphor and Symbolic Representation: The Image of God as a Suckling Mother in Thirteenth-Century Kabbalah." PhD. diss., University of Chicago, 2005.

Holtzer, Elie. "What Connects 'Good' Teaching, Text Study and Hevruta Learning? A Conceptual Argument." *Journal of Jewish Education* 7, no. 3 (2006): 183–204.

Hutner, R. Yitzhak. *Pahad Yitzhak: Hanukkah.* 4th edition. Jerusalem: Beit Midrash Pahad Yitzhak, 1995.

———. *Pahad Yitzhak: Iggerot u-Khetavim.* 3rd edition. Jerusalem: Beit Midrash Pahad Yitzhak, 1998.

Idel, Moshe. *"Ganz Andere:* On Rudolph Otto and Concepts of Holiness in Jewish Mysticism." *Da'at: A Journal of Jewish Philosophy and Kabbalah* 57–59 (2006): 5–44.

———. "George Steiner: Prophet of Abstraction." *Modern Judaism* 25, no. 2 (2005): 109–40.

———. *Golem: Jewish Magical and Mystical Traditions on the Artificial Anthropoid.* Albany, NY: SUNY Press, 1990.

———. "Models of Learning in Jewish Mysticism." Unpublished lecture at the Institute for Advanced Study, Hebrew University, Jerusalem, Summer 1998.

Jaffe, Martin. "A Rabbinic Ontology of the Written and Spoken Word: On Disciple-ship, Transformative Knowledge, and the Living Texts of Oral Torah." *Journal of the American Academy of Religion* 65, no. 3 (1997): 526–49.

———. *Torah in the Mouth: Writing and Oral Tradition in Palestinian Judaism, 200 BCE–400CE*. New York: Oxford University Press, 2001.

Johnson, David, and Roger Johnson. *Active Learning: Cooperation in the College Class-room*. Edina, MN: Interaction Book Company, 1991.

Kagan, Zipporah. "Divergent Tendencies and Their Literary Moulding in the Agga-dah." *Scripta Hierosolymitana* 12 (1971): 51–70.

Kahn, R. Aaron. *"Hadrat ha-Melekh": Al ha-Zikkah ha-Hadadit shel Rav ve-Talmid.* Beit Yosef Shaul: Kovetz Hiddushei Torah. Edited by Elchanan Asher Adler. New York: Gruss Kollel, Rabbi Isaac Elchanan Seminary, Yeshiva University, 1993.

Kanarfogel, Ephraim. *Jewish Education and Society in the High Middle Ages*. Detroit: Wayne State University Press, 1992.

Kenit, Ori. "Interactive Text Study: A Case of Hevruta Learning." *Journal of Jewish Education* 72, no. 3 (2006): 205–32.

Kerdeman, Deborah. "Some Thoughts about Hermeneutics and Jewish Religious Edu-cation." *Religious Education* 93, no. 1 (1998): 29–43.

Levinas, Emmanuel. *Difficult Freedom: Essays on Judaism*. Translated by Sean Hand. Baltimore: Johns Hopkins University Press, 1990.

———. *Nine Talmudic Readings*. Edited and translated by Annette Aronowicz. Bloom-ington: Indiana University Press, 1990.

———. *Otherwise Than Being, or Beyond Essence*. Translated by Alphonso Lingis. 1974. Reprint, The Hague: Martinus Nijhoff, 1981.

———. *Totality and Infinity*. Pittsburgh: Duquesne University Press, 1969.

Levinson, Joshua. "Enchanting Rabbi: Contest Narratives between Rabbi and Magi-cians in Late Antiquity." *Jewish Quarterly Review* 100, no. 1 (2010): 54–94.

Livsey, Rachel C., and Parker J. Palmer. *The Courage to Teach: A Guide for Reflection and Renewal*. San Francisco: Jossey-Bass, 1998.

Lukinsky, Joseph S. "Mentors, Colleagues, and Disciples." In *Educational Delibera-tions: Studies In Education Dedicated to Shlomo (Seymour) Fox*, edited by Mor-decai Nisan and Oded Schremer, 303–23. Jerusalem: Keter, Mandel Leadership Institute, 2005.

Luria, R. Rafael Moshe. *Beit Genazai: Amalut ba-Torah*. Jerusalem, n.p, 2002.

———. *Beit Genazai: Perushim al Massekhet Avot*. Jerusalem, n.p., 2002.

Maharal (R. Yehudah Loew ben Bezalel). *Be'er ha-Golah*. Benei Berak: Yahadut, 1980.

———. *Derekh Hayyim*. Benei Berak: Yahadut, 1980.

———. *Netivot Olam*. Benei Berak: Yahadut, 1980.

———. *Sefer Hiddushei Aggadot*. Benei Berak, 1980.

Marsden, George M. *The Outrageous Idea of Christian Scholarship*. New York: Oxford University Press, 1997.

———. *The Soul of the American University: From Protestant Establishment to Estab-lished Nonbelief*. New York: Oxford University Press, 1994.

Marrou, Henri Irénée. *History of Education in Antiquity*. New York: Sheed and Ward, 1956.

Midrash Rabbah, Vilna 1878. Reprint, Benei Berak: Makhon Or Torah 1997.

Midrash Tanhuma. Edited by Salomon Buber. Vilna: Romm, 1885.

Mishnayot Mevoarot. Edited by Pinkas Kohati. Jerusalem: Hemed, 1991.

Morris, Nathan. *Toledot ha-Hinnukh shel Am Yisrael*. 1930. Jerusalem: Rubin Mass, 1977.

Nisan, Mordecai, and Oded Schremer, eds. *Educational Deliberations: Studies in Education Dedicated to Shlomo (Seymour) Fox*. Jerusalem: Keter, Mandel Leadership Institute, 2005.

Nahman of Breslov. *Likkutei Moharan*. 1811. Jerusalem: Agudat Meshek Ha-Nahal, 1959.

——. *Sefer ha-Middot*. 1821. Warsaw, n.p., 1912.

Neusner, Jacob. *Rabbi Eliezer ben Hyrcanus*. Leiden: Brill, 1973.

Newman, Louis I. *Hasidic Anthology*. New York: Schocken Books, 1963.

Noam, Vered. "Bein Pulmus le-Mahaloket: Maddua Nuddah R. Eliezer?" *Massekhet* 5 (2006): 125–44.

O'Reilly, Mary Rose. *The Peaceable Classroom*. Portsmouth, NH: Boynton/Cook, 1993.

——. *Radical Presence Teaching as Contemplative Practice*. Portsmouth, NH: Boynton/Cook, 1998.

——. "Silence and Slow Time: Pedagogies from Inner Space." *Pre-Text* 11, nos. 1–2 (1990): 135–43.

Palmer, Parker. *The Courage to Teach: Exploring the Inner Landscape of a Teacher's Life*. San Francisco: Jossey-Bass, 1998.

——. *Let Your Life Speak: Listening to the Voice of Vocation*. San Francisco: Jossey-Bass, 2000.

——. *To Know as We Are Known: Education as a Spiritual Journey*. San Francisco: Harper, 1983.

Pirkei de-Rabbi Eliezer. Edited by M. Horowitz. Jerusalem: Makor, 1972.

Pirkei de-Rabbi Eliezer. Introduction by R. David Luria (Radal). Warsaw, 1852. Reprint, Jerusalem, n.p., 1963.

Rambam (R. Moses Maimonides). *The Guide for the Perplexed*. Translated by Maurice Friedlander. 2nd edition. New York: Dover, 1956.

——. *Mishneh Torah*. Standard printed edition. Jerusalem: Segulah, 2003.

——. *Perush ha-Mishnayot* [Commentary on the Mishnah]. Warsaw, n.p., 1878.

Ramhal (R. Moshe Hayyim Luzzatto). *KL'H Pithei Hokhmah*. Edited by Hayyim Friedlander. Benei Berak: Ahim Gitler, 2001.

Rashi (R. Shelomo ben Yitzhak). *Perushei ha-Torah*. Edited by Dov Shavell. Jerusalem: Mosad ha-Rav Kook, 1994.

Rosen, Gilla Ratzersdorfer. "Empathy and Aggression in Torah Study: Analysis of a Talmudic Description of *Havruta* Learning." In *Wisdom from All My Teachers: Challenges and Initiatives in Contemporary Torah Education*, edited by Susan Handelman and Jeffery Saks, 249–63. Jerusalem: Urim Press, 2003.

Rosenak, Michael. *Roads to the Palace: Jewish Texts and Teaching.* Oxford: Berghan Books, 1995.

Rosenblum, Jordan. *Food and Identity in Early Rabbinic Judaism.* Cambridge, UK: Cambridge University Press, 2010.

Rosenzweig, Franz. *The Star of Redemption.* 2nd edition. Translated by William Hallo. Notre Dame, IN: University of Notre Dame Press, 1985. Originally published 1930; New York: Holt Rhinehart, 1970.

———. *On Jewish Learning.* Edited by Nahum Glatzer. New York: Schocken, 1965. Originally published 1955.

Rubenstein, Jeffrey L. *The Culture of the Babylonian Talmud.* Baltimore: Johns Hopkins University Press, 2003.

———. "The Death of Rabbi Eliezer. *Sanhedrin* 68a." Unpublished manuscript.

———. *Stories of the Babylonian Talmud.* Baltimore: Johns Hopkins University Press, 2010.

———. *Talmudic Stories: Narrative Art, Composition, and Culture.* Baltimore: Johns Hopkins University Press, 1999.

Saks, Jeffrey. "Rabbi Joseph B. Soloveitchik and the Israeli Chief Rabbinate: Biographical Notes, 1959–60 (*B.D.D.*)." *Be-Khol Derakhekha Da'ehu* 17 (2006): 45–67.

Schachter-Shalomi, Zalman. *Spiritual Intimacy: A Study of Counseling in Hasidism.* New Jersey: Jason Aronson, 1991.

Scharfstein, Zvi. *Toledot ha-Hinnukh be-Yisrael ba-Dorot ha-Aharonim.* Jerusalem: Rubin Mass, 1960.

Schechter, Solomon, ed. *Avot de-Rabbi Natan.* New York: Jewish Theological Seminary, 1967. Originally published 1887.

Scheffler, Israel. *Teachers of My Youth: An American Jewish Experience.* Dordrecht: Kluwer Academic Publishers, 1995.

Schneersohn, R. Yosef Yitzhak. *Kelalei ha-Hinnukh ve-ha-Hadrakhah.* Kefar Habad, n.p., 2000. *The Principles of Education and Guidance.* Translated by Y. Danziger. New York: Kehot Publication Society, 1990. Originally published 1944.

Scholes, Robert. *Textual Power: Literary Theory and the Teaching of English.* New Haven: Yale University Press, 1986.

———. *The Rise and Fall of English.* New Haven: Yale University Press, 1998.

Schwab, Joseph. "Eros and Education." In *Science, Curriculum, and Liberal Education: Selected Essays*, edited by Ian Westbury and Neil Wilkof, 105–32. Chicago: University of Chicago Press, 1978.

Schwehn, Mark. *Exiles from Eden: Religion and the Academic Vocation in America.* New York: Oxford University Press, 1992.

Segal, Aliza. *Hevruta Study: History, Benefits, and Enhancements.* Jerusalem: ATID, Academy for Torah Initiatives and Directions, 2003.

Segal, Eliezer. "Law as Allegory? An Unnoticed Literary Device in Talmudic Narratives." *Prooftexts* 8 (1988): 245–56.

Shapira, R. Kalman Klonymous. *A Student's Obligation: Advice from the Rebbe of the Warsaw Ghetto.* Translated by Micha Odenheimer. New Jersey: Jason Aronson, 1995.

———. *Hakhsharat ha-Avrekhim.* Jerusalem, n.p., 1965.

———. *To Heal the Soul: The Spiritual Journey of a Chasidic Rebbe.* Translated by Yehoshua Starret. New Jersey: Jason Aronoson, 1995.

Shulman, Lee S. *Communities of Learners and Communities of Teachers.* Jerusalem: Mandel Institute, 1997.

———. "Theory, Practice, and the Education of Professionals." *The Elementary School Journal* 98, no. 5 (1998): 511–26.

Soloveitchik, Hayyim. "Rupture and Redemption: The Transformation of Contemporary Orthodoxy." *Tradition* 28, no. 4 (1994): 64–131.

Soloveitchik, Rabbi Joseph B. *And From There You Shall Seek.* Translated by Naomi Goldblum. New York: Ktav, 2009.

———. "On the Love of Torah and the Redemption of This Generation's Soul." Hebrew: *"Al Ahavat ha-Torah u-Geulat Nefesh ha-Dor."* Jerusalem: Department for Torah Education and Culture for the Diaspora, 1992.

———. "Ha-Yehudi Mashul le-Sefer Torah." In *Beit Yosef Shaul: Kovetz Hiddushei Torah,* edited by Elchanan Asher Adler, 68–100. New York: Gruss Kollel, Rabbi Isaac Elchanan Seminary, Yeshiva University, 1993.

———. *The Halakhic Mind: An Essay on Jewish Tradition and Modern Thought.* 1944. Reprint, New York: Free Press, 1986.

———. *Nefesh ha-Rav.* Edited by Hershel Schachter. Jerusalem: Reishit Yerushalyim, 1994.

———. "Teaching with Clarity and Empathy." In *Reflections of the Rav: Lessons in Jewish Thought,* vol. 1, edited by Avraham Besdin, 150–59. Hoboken, NJ: Ktav, 1979.

Stampfer, Shaul. *Ha-Yeshivah ha-Litait be-Hithavutah.* Jerusalem: Zalman Shazar, 1955.

Steiner, George. *Lessons of the Masters.* Cambridge, MA: Harvard University Press, 2003.

Stone, Suzanne. "In Pursuit of the Counter-text: The Turn to the Jewish Legal Model in Contemporary American Legal Theory." *Harvard Law Review* 106 (1993): 813–94.

Talmud Bavli [Babylonian Talmud]. Standard printed edition, Romm: Vilna 1886.

Talmud Yerushalmi [Palestinian Jerusalem Talmud]. Standard printed edition based on the 1st edition Venice, 1523, Piotrkow 1898–1900.

Tanna de-Bei Eliyahu. Standard printed edition. Jerusalem: Eshkol, 1993.

Tanna de-Bei Eliyahu. Translated by William Braude and Israel Kapstein. Philadelphia: Jewish Publication Society, 1981.

Tishby, Isaiah, and Fischel Lachower, eds. *The Wisdom of the Zohar: An Anthology of Texts.* Translated by David Goldstein. Oxford: Oxford University Press, 1989.

Tompkins, Jane. *A Life in School: What the Teacher Learned.* Boston, MA: Addison-Wesley, 1996.

———. "Pedagogy of the Distressed." *College English* 10 (1990): 653–60.

Torat Hayyim: Hamishah Humshei Torah. Edited by M. Katzenellenbogen. Jerusalem: Mossad ha-Rav Kook, 1986.

Vilna Ga'on (Eliyahu ben Shelomo). *Perush al Shir ha-Shirim*. In *Mikra'ot Gedolot*: *Urim Gedolim, Hamesh Megillot*. Jerusalem: Even Yisrael, 1949.

———. *Perush al-Sefer Mishlei*. Jerusalem: Even Yisrael, 1993.

Volozhin, R. Hayyim. *Nefesh ha-Hayyim*. Edited by Y.D. Rubin. Benei Berak, n.p., 1988. Originally published 1873.

Wiskind-Elper, Ora. *Tradition and Fantasy in the Tales of Reb Nahman of Bratslav*. Albany: SUNY Press, 1998.

———. *Wisdom of the Heart: The Teachings of Rabbi Ya'akov of Izbica-Radzyn*. Philadelphia: Jewish Publication Society, 2010.

Yalkut Shimoni Midrash al-ha-Torah. Nevi'im u-Khetuvim. Standard printed edition.

Yerushalmi, Yosef Hayim. *Zakhor: Jewish History and Jewish Memory*. Seattle: University of Washington Press, 1983.

Ziegler, Reuven. Online lecture series on the thought of R. Joseph B. Soloveitchik. http://www.vbm-torah.org/archives/ravindex.htm.

Zohar: The Pritzker Edition. Translated by Daniel Matt. Palo Alto, CA: Stanford University Press, 2003–.

Zohar. 2nd edition. Translated by Harry Sperling and Maurice Simon. London: Soncino Press, 1984.

INDEX

A

Abba Shaul, 24

Abba Sikra, 19

Abel (in Genesis), 93, 129n40

Abraham (in Genesis), 129–30n40

Adam (in Genesis), 111n10

Adelman, Rachel, 28

aggadah, 11, 44, 49, 90

Akhnai, 51. *See also* "Oven of Akhnai," story of

Akiva, R.: and Bar Kokhba, 71, 72, 118n13; death of, 30, 71–72, 91; in "Oven of Akhnai," 42, 53–54, 68, 75; parable on teaching, 125n9; in R. Eliezer's passing, 62–65, 71–72, 78, 91, 93–94, 124n4; and Roman occupation, 4, 100–101, 132n6; and sorcery, 62, 95; in Yavneh, 50, 83; in *Zohar*, 129n39

Alter, Robert, 73

Amazing Adventures of Kavalier & Clay, The. See Chabon, Michael

am ha-aretz. See people of the land (*am ha-aretz*)

Amital, R. Yehudah, 58–59

amulet, 64, 86

Arakh, R. Eleazar ben. *See* Eleazar, R.

Arendt, Hannah, 10–11

arms, R. Eliezer's, 21, 63, 74–75

Askénazi, R. Léon: on Abel and Cain, 129n40; on body and spirit, 111n10; on education, 92–93; on food, 29; on Jewish versus Greek philosophical modes, 114n21; and Levinas, 82, 107n8; on Oral versus Written Torah, 7–9; on Pharisees, 82–83; and post–World War II French Jewry, 107n8; and "return to Hebrew," 108n21; and R. Yitzhak Hutner, 107n10; on teachers, 18, 115n21

Auerbach, Erich, 28

B

Babylonian Talmud: and R. Ze'eira, 33; on sorcery, 79; versus Jerusalem Talmud, 33, 62, 124n3

ball, 64, 86, 89

banning (*niddui*): and excommunication (*herem*), 53, 70; laws of, 70, 119–20n18; and purity/impurity, 87; of R. Eliezer, 21, 42, 53, 56; and R. Eliezer's passing, 62, 66, 68, 69, 75, 86; revocation of, 64, 89, 90–91, 95

Bar Kokhba (rebellion), 50, 71, 72, 118n13

bat kol. See heavenly voice

bed, canopied (*kinof*), 63, 65–66

be'er ("well"), 25. *See also* spring

beginnings, story of R. Eliezer's, 21–23, 26–38; compared to death of Moses, 103; compared to Elijah and Elisha, 92; compared to "Oven of Akhnai," 52; compared to passing, 64–65, 67; isolation in, 27

Elijah the Prophet (2 Kings): death of, 103; and R. Eliezer, 61, 91–93; and teacher/student relation, 100

Eliot, T.S., 89–90

Elisha (in 2 Kings): and death of Elijah, 103; and Elijah (2:21), 61, 92; and teacher/student relation, 100

Eliyahu, R. (Ga'on of Vilna), 35, 104

enclothing, 14

Enlightenment, 81

eros: Freud ("life instinct"), 79; of knowledge, 29; man and God, 35; in Song of Songs, 113n16

Essenes, 82

"Ethics of the Fathers." *See Pirkei Avot*

excommunication (*herem*), 53, 70, 119–20n18

Exodus, book of: death of Moses in (34:28), 104; midrash on "drop of ink" (47:6), 98; in "Oven of Akhnai" (23:2), 42, 56, 58; and tefillin (13:9, 31:17), 124n4; "two tablets" (31:18), 6–7, 9

Ezekiel, book of, 129n39

F

"falling on the face," 43, 53, 56

famine, 19, 28

father: R. Eliezer's (*see* Hyrcanus); and son relation, 26–28, 67. *See also* parent/child relation

final lament, R. Eliezer's, 16, 21, 27–28, 63, 76, 98

Fisch, Menachem, 128n34

food: metaphor of, 27–32, 113n12; R. Askénazi on, 111n10. *See also* hunger

Fortinbras (in *Hamlet*), 94

Fraenkel, Yonah, 66, 69, 124n3

Freud, Sigmund, 5; critique of, 82; and dreams, 49; and *thanatos* and *eros*, 79

Frost, Robert, 13

G

Gamaliel, Rabban: and banning R. Eliezer, 68, 71, 127–28n34; "Find

yourself a teacher," 115n21; in "Oven of Akhnai," 42–43, 53, 55, 56

Ga'on of Vilna (R. Eliyahu), 35, 104

Genesis, book of: Abel and Cain, 93, 129n40; Adam, 111n10; and Kabbalah, 120n21

German universities, 3, 5

gestures, 74–75

God: assistance from, 59; as Creator, 120n21, 130n45; and Elijah, 92; as father, 28, 60; grace of, 113n12; and humanity, 73, 127n26; and interpretation, 119n15; and Israel, 7, 124n4, 125n11; living (versus dead), 58; love of, 35, 113n16; and Moses, 9, 38, 101–4, 112n12; name of, 115n21; and *ona'at devarim*, 56; and relation to world, 10, 48; return to, 40; smile of, 42, 56, 60, 85; as teacher (of Moses), 6–7; and tefillin, 73; and Torah, 52, 85; unity with, 99; word of, 8, 38

Golem, 83, 130n45

Gordin, Jacob, 108–9n21

Greenwood, Daniel, 57, 60

"Great Revolt," 18–20, 43

ground, 42, 52–53, 91

H

Ha-Ari (R. Yitzhak Luria), 96

Hadrian (emperor), 50, 71

halakhah: and death, 80; in "Oven of Akhnai," 41–42, 58, 96; Soloveitchik on, 126n22; in Talmud, 44, 90; teacher/student relation in, 11–12

Hama, R. Pinhas ben, 9

Hamlet (Shakespeare): Hamlet on death, 79; Hamlet's funeral, 93–94; Polonius, 12; T.S. Eliot on, 89–90

Hananiah, R. Yehoshua ben. *See* Yehoshua, R.

Hanina, R. (son of R. Idi), 41

havruta, 7, 16, 106–7n5

Hayyim, R. (of Brisk), 80

Hayyim, R. Yosef (Chief Rabbi of Baghdad). *See* Ben Ish Hai heavenly voice (*bat kol*): Maharal on, 131n46; in "Oven of Akhnai," 41–42, 56, 59, 121n23, 123n25

Heidegger, Martin, 81

Heiman, R. Shlomo, 13

Heller, R. Hayyim, 132n3

Hellner-Eshed, Melila, 31–32, 35

Henkin, R. Yosef Eliyahu, 49–51, 72

herem. See excommunication

hermeneutic circle, 118–19n15

Hisda, R., 36–37, 41, 55

history (*toledot*), 49

holiness, 80–81, 106n5. *See also* holy

Holocaust, 79, 81

holy (*kadosh*): Moshe Idel on, 127n26; and Pharisees, 80, 83. *See also* holiness

house of study (*beit midrash*). *See* study house

hunger, 27–32. *See also* food

Hutner, R. Yitzhak: on food and learning, 112–13n12; on Maharal, 107–8n13; on Oral Torah versus Western tradition, 107–8n13; on Oral versus Written Torah, 107n9; and R. Askénazi, 107n10;

Hyrcanus (father of R. Eliezer), 22–23, 28, 32, 36–37

Hyrcanus, R. Eliezer ben. *See* Eliezer, R.

Hyrcanus (son of R. Eliezer), 63, 66–69

I

Idel, Moshe: on books and learning, 5–6; on Golem, 130n45; on holiness, 127n26

illusion. *See* sorcery

Imma Shalom (wife of R. Eliezer): literal meaning of, 55; in "Oven of Akhnai," 42–43, 54–57, 123n26

impurity (*tumah*): and dead bodies, 45–46, 68, 79, 84; in "Oven of Akhnai," 58, 60; in rituals, 44, 116n7. *See also tumah* and *taharah*

Isaiah, book of: God's leading in (48:17), 59; wise men and knowledge (44:25), 118n14

Israel: chariot and horsemen, 61, 64, 91–92; and God, 7, 123n4, 125n11; Moses as teacher of, 101–2; political sovereignty of, 51. *See also* Land of Israel

"It is not in heaven": current debate on, 123n26; in Deuteronomy (30:12), 39–40; in "Oven of Akhnai," 42, 55–56, 59–60, 90, 117n8, 121n21

J

Jaffee, Martin, 125–26n16

James, Henry, 12

Jerusalem: contemporary city of, 4; in R. Eliezer's beginnings, 22–23, 27, 29, 32; Roman siege of, 28, 36, 50, 83, 118n14. *See also* Temple

Jerusalem Talmud: versus Babylonian, 33, 62; and Bar Kokhba, 118n13; version of R. Eliezer's passing, 66, 70

K

Kabbalah, 44, 113n13, 115n21, 120n21

kadosh. See holy

Kafka, Franz, "The Hunger Artist," 28

Kahn, R. Aaron, 103, 133n6

Keats, John, 13

keli. See vessel

Kelim (Mishnah), 45–48, 87, 116n7

keri'ah, 4, 6

Kierkegaard, Søren, 108n20

Kings, 1 book of (1:19), 92

Kings, 2 book of: death of Elijah in (2:9–10), 103; Elijah and chariot (2:11–12), 61, 92; in R. Eliezer's passing (2:12), 64, 91; teacher/student relation in (3:11), 100

kinof ("canopied bed"), 63, 65

kiss, 9–10, 38

kohen (Temple priest), 83

Kohen, R. Tzadok ha- (R. Tzadok), 59

Kohen, R. Yose ha-, 24

Kokhba, Shimon bar. *See* Bar Kokhba (rebellion)

Kook, R. Avraham Yitzhak, 110n4
Kujavski, R. Marc, 116–17n8, 120–21n21

L

Lakish, R. Shimon ben, 98
Lamentations, book of (3:8), 41
Landes, R. Daniel, 34
Land of Israel: independence of (1948), 20, 51; Roman occupation, 4; in R. Ze'eira's story, 33. *See also* Israel
Lear (in *King Lear*), 54
Leibush, R. Meir ben Yechiel Michel (Malbim), 116n5, 117–18n11
leprosy, 63, 78
Levi, R., 9
Levinas, Emmanuel: on purity/impurity, 80–83; and R. Askénazi, 82, 107n8; on R. Eliezer's passing, 12–13, 65, 94, 95; on R. Eliezer as teacher, 76; on sorcery, 78–79, 127n26
Leviticus, book of: and leprosy (13:2), 63, 78; on sacrifices, 111n10
life instinct (*eros*), 79
literary theory, 15, 108n20; and pedagogy, 109n22
love: learning of Torah, 34–35; and teaching, 10; in Song of Songs, 113n16. *See also* eros
Luria, R. David (Radal), 116n5
Luria, R. Yitzhak (Ha-Ari), 96
Lydda, 64, 91

M

ma'ayan ("wellspring"), 24–25. *See also* spring
ma'ayanot, 35. *See also* spring
magic. *See* sorcery
Maharal of Prague (R. Yehudah Loew ben Bezalel), 83, 107–8n13, 131n46
Maharsha (R. Shemuel Eidels), 53
Maimonides, Moses, 53, 110n5, 133n6
Malbim (R. Meir Leibush ben Yechiel Michel), 116n5, 117–18n11
Marxism, 82

Meir, R., 130n43, 132n6
Meir, R. Ya'akov ben. *See* Rabbenu Tam
Messianic Era, 96
methodology, 11–17, 64
midrash. *See specific texts*
midwife, 114n21
milk, 30, 112n11
Miller, R. Chaim, 121–22n23
Mishnah: R. Eliezer cited in, 59; on "Oven of Akhnai," 47; and ritual purity, 116n7; on "Vessels" (*Kelim*), 45–48
Modern Orthodoxy (in America), 98–99
Molkho, R. Shelomo, 43
money changer, 64, 91, 94
Moses: death of, 101–4; in "drop of ink" midrash, 98; as father, 28; and God, 9, 38, 101–4, 112n12; and R. Eliezer's beginnings, 103; as student (of God), 6–7
Mother of Peace: 55, 57. *See also* Imma Shalom
Mothers, Torah of, 55
Mount Sinai: midrash on Exodus (31:18), 9; in "Oven of Akhnai," 42, 56; and R. Eliezer's stone, 20; revelation at, 6–7, 9. *See also* Sinai
mouth: of God, 7, 9; kiss, 9–10, 38; "People of the," 4; "the piece which is in your," 9; R. Eliezer's open (*petah*), 33–34; stone in R. Eliezer's, 22, 27, 29; Torah of the (*see* Oral Torah)

N

Nahman of Bratslav, R., 14–15, 17
Nahman, R. Yehudah bar, 98
Nahmani, R. Shemuel bar, 74, 102
Nakdimon ben Guryon, 23, 32, 36
Nasi, R. Yehudah ha–, 132n6
Nathaniel, R. Shimon ben, 24
Nazis, 11, 81, 82
Negative Capability, 13
Néher, Andre, 107n8
Neuman, Yair, 118–19n15
niddui. *See* banning

118n13; against Rome, 18–20, 43, 50, 83
Rich, Adrienne, "Cartographies of
    Silence," 34
Romans: destruction wrought by, 38;
    "Great Revolt" against, 18–20, 43;
    imprisonment of Akiva, 100; occu-
    pation of Jerusalem, 4, 50, 71, 83,
    100–101, 132n6
Romanticism, 89
Rorschach (image), 43
Rosenzweig, Franz, 3–4, 15, 113n16
Rubenstein, Jeffrey, 52

S

Sabbath: and prohibitions, 67–68, 123n4;
    in R. Eliezer's beginnings, 22, 27; in R.
    Eliezer's passing, 63, 64, 66, 91
sacrifices, 44, 111n10
Sadducees, 82
Sages: fire of the, 39; and interpretation,
    119n15; and laws, 44; and Oral Torah,
    125–26n16; in "Oven of Akhnai," 41,
    43, 57–60, 121n21, 122n23; in Proverbs
    (22:18), 18; on purity, 47, 86–90; after
    R. Eliezer's passing, 97; in R. Eliezer's
    passing, 63, 65, 67, 69–71, 128n37;
    Roman occupation, 4, 71; and sorcery,
    73–74, 84; *talmid hakham* (highly
    learned Sage), 114n21; and Torah,
    52; in Yavneh, 20, 128n34; in *Zohar*,
    129n39. *See also specific names*
Saks, Jeffery, 74
salon (*teraklin*), 63, 65
scale, 24, 26, 93
Schneersohn, R. Menachem M.,
    121–22n23
Scripture, 8
scroll(s). *See under* Torah
Segal, Eliezer, 128n35
Seth (in Genesis), 129n40
Shalom, Imma. *See* Imma Shalom
Shammua, R. Eleazar ben, 130n43,
    132–33n6
shevut, 63, 67

shoe: in R. Eliezer's passing, 64, 86,
    88–89, 128–29n35, 128n37; and synec-
    doche, 90
shoe-form. *See* shoe
silence, 33–34
Sinai: as father, 28; revelation at, 6–7,
    131n46. *See also* Mount Sinai
Six-Day War, 51
snake: and hermeneutic circle, 118–19n15;
    and Oral Torah, 51; in "Oven of Akh-
    nai," 41, 47, 118n14
Socrates. *See* Plato
Soloveitchik, R. Joseph B.: on "drop of ink"
    midrash, 98; on fear of death, 79–80;
    on *halakhah*, 126n22; on Moses,
    112n12; on Oral v, Written Torah,
    106n5; on R. Eliezer's final lament and
    Oral Torah, 16; on teacher/student
    relation, 6, 98–100, 101; on teaching
    Torah and childhood, 99–100, 132n3
Song of Songs, 113n16, 129n39; kisses
    (1:2), 9
sorcery: and death, 79; and laws of purity/
    impurity, 84–85; and Oral Torah, 62,
    85; and R. Eliezer's passing, 62, 64,
    73, 77–83, 94–96; and Sages, 73–74;
    and teachers, 95. *See also* cucumbers
    (magic)
spot, deep bright (leprosy), 63, 78
spring (*ma'ayanot*): metaphor of, 24–26,
    29, 34, 52; in Proverbs (5:15–16), 18, 35;
    teachers as, 103
stick, painting, 16, 21, 63, 76–77
stone: in R. Eliezer's mouth, 22, 27, 29; R.
    Eliezer's sitting, 20; significance of,
    30–31
study house (*beit midrash*): atmosphere
    in, 7; in "Oven of Akhnai," 41, 58, 96
    123n26
suckling, 30, 101

T

taharah and *tumah*. See *tumah* and
    taharah

tahor ("clean"): in "Oven of Akhnai," 41, 47; in R. Eliezer's passing, 60, 62, 64, 88, 89, 121n21

Talmud: editors of, 13, 49; interpretations of, 44; Oral versusWritten Torah, 7; R. Eliezer cited in, 59

tame' (unclean): in "Oven of Akhnai," 41, 46; in R. Eliezer's passing, 64, 86–87; and shoe, 129n37. See also *tumah* and *taharah*

teacher/student relation: Askénazi on, 115n21; cistern and spring metaphor, 25–26; Elijah and Elisha, 92; and food, 30; God and Israel, 7; and interpretation, 40; intimacy in, 10, 75, 100–101; and Oral Torah, 6; and "Oven of Akhnai," 48, 57; and parent/child, 11, 26, 96; in Proverbs (5:15–16), 35; in rabbinic literature, 11; reciprocity in, 132–33n6; and R. Eliezer's passing, 72

teaching texts, 14

tears, 41, 42, 54, 55

tefillin (phylacteries): prohibition of, 124n4; in R. Eliezer's passing, 63, 66–67; symbolic meaning of, 73

Temple (of Jerusalem): destruction of (70 CE), 20, 39, 44–45, 50, 111–12n10; in "Oven of Akhnai," 41, 43, 55, 121n21; and Pharisees, 82; and purity/impurity, 80; sacrifices in, 44–45, 111n10; and Zealots, 83

Ten Commandments, 6–7, 9

teraklin ("salon"), 63, 65

thanatos ("death instinct"), 79

Thomas, Dylan, 66

Tillich, Paul, 14

time, 66

toledot ("history"), 49

Torah: American students of, 99; and God, 52; Hebrew word, 4–5; interpretive authority of, 48; "It is not in heaven," 39–40, 42, 56, 59–60, 85, 90; and Moses, 98; of the mouth (*see* Oral Torah); scroll(s), 16, 21, 63, 74–75, 89;

as vessel, 121n21. *See also* Oral Torah; Written Torah

Trajan (emperor), 50

truth: and "Oven of Akhnai," 57–59, 85, 123n25; in R. Eliezer's beginnings, 23, 25, 28, 33, 38

tumah and *taharah*, laws concerning: and dead bodies, 45, 46, 68, 79, 84; Levinas on, 80–83, 127n26; in Mishnah, 116n7; and "Oven of Akhnai," 45–48, 116–17n8, 117–18n11, 120–21n21; in R. Eliezer's passing, 64, 86–90, 91, 129n37; R. Eliezer versus Yehoshua on, 122n24; and shoe, 88–89; and sorcery, 84–85; and Temple, 83; and vessels, 87. *See also* impurity; purity

Tzadok, R. (Tzadok ha–Kohen), 59

tzimtzum ("contraction"), 120n21

V

Vespasian (emperor): and R. Yohanan, 50, 118n14; siege of Jerusalem, 20, 36

vessel (*keli*): cistern, 25; and *Malkhut*, 113n13; and R. Eliezer's passing, 128n37; Torah as, 120–21n21. See also *Kelim* (Mishnah)

violence, 81–82

voice from heaven. *See* heavenly voice

Volozhin, R. Hayyim, 10

W

weight, small, 64, 86

well (*be'er*), 25. *See also* spring

wellspring (*ma'ayan*), 25. *See also* spring

Wiskind-Elper, Ora, 87, 112n11, 129n37

Written Torah, 4–9, 16, 38, 46, 106n5, 126n16

Wordsworth, William, *Preface to the Lyrical Ballads*, 89

World War II: Levinas and, 81; Modern Orthodoxy after (in America), 99; French Jewry after, 82, 107n8

THE SAMUEL AND ALTHEA STROUM LECTURES IN JEWISH STUDIES

The Yiddish Art Song
performed by Leon Lishner, basso, and Lazar Weiner, piano (stereophonic record album)

The Holocaust in Historical Perspective
Yehuda Bauer

Zakhor: Jewish History and Jewish Memory
Yosef Hayim Yerushalmi

Jewish Mysticism and Jewish Ethics
Joseph Dan

The Invention of Hebrew Prose: Modern Fiction and the Language of Realism
Robert Alter

Recent Archaeological Discoveries and Biblical Research
William G. Dever

Jewish Identity in the Modern World
Michael A. Meyer

I. L. Peretz and the Making of Modern Jewish Culture
Ruth R. Wisse

The Kiss of God: Spiritual and Mystical Death in Judaism
Michael Fishbane

Gender and Assimilation in Modern Jewish History:
The Roles and Representation of Women
Paula E. Hyman